SAMSON

SAMSON

THE SECRET
OF
STRENGTH

PHIL STANTON

Cook Communications

Victor is an imprint of
Cook Communications Ministries, Colorado Springs, Colorado 80918
Cook Communications, Paris, Ontario
Kingsway Communications, Eastbourne, England

SAMSON: THE SECRET OF STRENGTH
© 1996 by Phil Stanton.
First U.S. edition, 2000
Printed in the United States of America.

Editor: Melissa Borger
Cover Design: Image Studios
Cover Photography: Cyberphoto/DigitalVision

1 2 3 4 5 6 7 8 9 10 Printing/Year 04 03 02 01 00

Unless otherwise noted biblical quotations are taken from *The New King James Version.* © 1979, 1980, 1982, Thomas Nelson, Inc., Publishers.

Library of Congress Ctaloging-in-Publication Data

Stanton, Phil, 1951–
    Samson: the secret of strength/Phil Stanton.—1st U.S. ed.
      p. cm.
    Originally published: Eastbourne, England: Kingsway
    Communications, © 1996.
    ISBN 1-56476-715-9
      1. Samson (Biblical judge) 2. Bible. O.T.—Biography. I. Title.

BS580.S15 S73 2000
222'.32092—dc21   00—031576

To my wife and my mother;
to Tony Williams
and Ray Bodkin—

thanks!

The *Chariot Victor Bible Character* series introduces us to people in the Bible and shows how their lives have much to teach us today. All the authors in the series use their communication skills to lead us through the biblical record and apply its encouragement and challenges to our lives today.

CONTENTS

RIDDLE UPON RIDDLE

Judges 13–16; Hebrews 11:32-39

Riddle is piled upon riddle in the story of Samson. What sort of a man was he? Why is his story so important for today? Our first impression of him may be this: he is a man of muscle, more brawn than brain. The Holy Spirit, it seems, gave him great physical strength, and little else. Does his life seem very carnal to you? "Take away the miracles," some might say, "and you're left with an unrestrained womanizer, living simply to serve his appetites."

But the Holy Spirit sees Samson very differently. He is listed with the great heroes of faith. The heroes' roll in Hebrews 11 names Samson with other men of faith who "through faith subdued kingdoms, worked righteousness, obtained promises, stopped the mouths of lions, quenched the violence of fire, escaped the edge of the sword, out of weakness were made strong, became valiant in battle, turned to flight the armies of the aliens" (Heb. 11:32-34).

Samson certainly did these things. He achieved them, the Spirit says, "through faith," and hence became a pattern for *our* lives.

It seems strange to think of Samson as a hero of faith. But

this is the Holy Spirit's last word on the man. We shall never understand him without it.

So, we have a task ahead of us: to see Samson as he really was. Very often, where there are apparent contradictions in the Bible, it is a sign for us to go deeper. In resolving the contradictions, we are led into spiritual mysteries. The harder the challenge of apparent contradictions, the greater the reward, when we study the Word of God. This happens when we study Samson.

What was the secret of Samson's strength? This seems no secret on first reading: it was his *hair*. Didn't the Philistines learn the secret, and didn't they use it to defeat Samson? Well, no—as we shall see.

What was Samson really like?

Here's another riddle: why do we disdain Samson, while the world admired him so? For the world *did* admire him.

In the ancient world, great and heroic people were viewed as gods. Around these "divine" figures, striking and heroic stories gathered from many sources. Now we know that the strong man-hero of the ancient world was Hercules. In the myths, Hercules was a semi-divine figure, who had many adventures. What true stories lie behind the myths that we know? It would be impossible to say, except for one thing: parts of the Hercules myth coincide with stories we know to be true—the heroic deeds of Samson.

The parallels are striking:

1. Names: "Samson" means "*sun*like." Hercules "is clearly a sun-god."[1]

2. Samson's first mighty deed was to kill a lion barehanded. Likewise, the first of Hercules' famous twelve tasks was to kill the mighty lion of Nemea. The lion skin became his trademark.

3. Samson married twice (as we shall see), and we see him

visiting a prostitute. Hercules also married twice. Like Samson, his first wife was killed, and his second betrayed him.

4. Samson became a slave, briefly, at the end of his life. Hercules too was a slave, for one year.

5. Samson's greatest feat was tearing apart two pillars; and Hercules is famous for his pillars. In one story, he tore apart the two rocks at the mouth of the Mediterranean—the "pillars of Hercules"—to let in the ocean.

Of course, there are aspects of the Hercules myth that have no origin in Samson. But the similarities cannot be mere coincidence. What then? I feel sure that the myth must have drawn from the actual facts of Samson's life.[2] Think for a moment what this means: Samson's deeds made such an impact that they became famous throughout the world. Of course, the vital aspects of the story—the things that God emphasizes in His Word—are not in the myth! But the man impressed his world so much that they couldn't forget him.

Why did he fascinate his world so much—and us so little?

Perhaps you can solve the mystery immediately. "Samson was a good fighter," you say, "and a womanizer. No wonder people were impressed." But far from solving the riddle, this only increases it. A sinful world wants to admire sinful people—why choose one of God's heroes of faith?

Are we fair to Samson? I don't think we are. David is a favorite character in the Old Testament, far dearer to most of us than Samson. But was David so different from Samson? Actually, their stories are strikingly similar.

Both felt the power of God first in killing lions. Both came to prominence by killing Philistines. Both had to kill Philistines to fulfill their wedding obligations: Samson killed thirty (Judg. 14:19), David 200 (twice as many as he needed to, (1 Sam. 18:27). Both became famous for the numbers they killed

("David has slain his ten thousands," 1 Sam. 18:7).

Both married women whose fathers broke the marriage covenant and gave their daughters to other men. After that, women were the weak point of both. We shall see Samson visit a prostitute. But was David any better? He had many wives, contrary to God's Word (see Deut. 17:17). And it was David who committed adultery with Bathsheba, and then had her husband killed to cover his crime.

Why then do we love David so much? It is because we see David's *inner* life—it is laid bare in the Psalms. We see his struggles, his anguish, his faith, his holy desires. We see his soul, and we love him.

What was Samson's inner life like? The Holy Spirit hides it from us. We haven't the faintest hint. But if we *could* see it, would it be so different from David's? If their *outer* lives were so strikingly parallel, why not their inner?

What was the secret of his strength?
This at least seems no riddle: it was in his hair, because, when it was cut off, Samson lost his strength. This is what the Philistines thought. But the Philistines were to discover (too late) that they were wrong.

As well as cutting off his hair, they blinded him. This was their moment of triumph. But we see in retrospect that, in blinding Samson, the Philistines sealed their own doom. Samson's eyes were the Philistines' only protection, and without them, they were defenseless.

For some of the Philistine officers, it is their first chance to see the famous hero up close. Many who have come this near have not lived to tell the tale. But they have seen him before: powerful, triumphant, undaunted by weight of enemies.

It is a different man they see now. At first he was furiously frustrated by the weakness of his body. He had expected his usual strength, and it had not come. Then he had realized that he would not be able to escape. An awful black gloom had settled on him.

The Philistines had enjoyed telling him how easily he had been tricked. He had not answered, but so powerful is his soul that they could almost *see* the emotion that now filled him. It is a disgusted and bitter regret.

He is a warrior, and has faced sudden death before. But the Philistines have something worse in store for him. Already a fire is blazing, heating the iron. The Philistines have been defeated so often by this man that they want to drain their victory to the dregs. They watch him closely as they say that he will be a slave for the rest of his life.

And he will be blinded. They draw his attention to the red-hot iron in the fire.

They await his reaction with happy anticipation.

And they are not disappointed. Not really—no man can face lifelong slavery with anything but horror. And being blinded produces all the agony and anguish that the spectators could wish.

But something is missing. Alongside the pain, regret, and horror, there is something else. They sense that the powerless captive has embraced a secret hope. When he heard that he would lose his eyes, something flickered in his soul.

The Philistines are determined to enjoy their moment of victory. Now is the time to put aside all their old fears. What is there to fear in a blind slave? Loud is their laughter; cheerful are their voices. And their noise covers the faint disquiet that rises in their hearts.

The hero is not about to voice his new hope. He has been a fool—a blind, sinful fool! He richly deserves death—and worse. But he is to live on, blinded.

Blinded!—behind the pain that engulfs him, he knows what it means. It is the Lord's mercy. Thinking to enjoy their victory to the full, the Philistines have removed their one defense. It is they who are blind!

Now, at last, he will fulfill his calling.

Perhaps the reader has not yet seen why Samson's eyes were the Philistines' protection. And perhaps he cannot fathom the riddle of Samson's strength. The answers will emerge as the story unfolds. We shall look for the clues where they lie waiting to be gathered. And it is vital we gather them! The secret of our own strength is here too.

How does all this apply to us?

Of course, the whole Bible applies to us. "Man shall live by *every* word that proceeds from the mouth of God" (Matt. 4:4). "Live by," Jesus says. On the physical level, we live by food, light, and air. Our souls require heavenly food. God's word *is* that food. We live in Christ *by* that word, as the Spirit opens our eyes to it.

Samson's story is a dark episode for many. But if the Spirit sheds His light on it, we shall find it contains a part of our essential diet.

The man we disdained will be seen as the hero he was. At last he found the secret of strength. It is a secret we too long to unveil. What better way than to follow, in the light of God's Word, a man who found that secret!

And our reward? The secret of strength for today!

----

1. The *Encyclopedia Britannica*, 11th edition, Vol. 13, article on "Hercules."
2. For examples of how biblical characters reappear in pagan myths, see John Owen's *Biblical Theology* 1661, English translation © 1994 *Soli Deo Gloria*.

THE IMPORTANCE OF BEING DIFFERENT

Judges 13:24–14:1

When Samson saw the woman of Timnah, two worlds collided. The woman was a Philistine, Samson an Israelite. Both are a fascinating study. Studying the Philistines means studying our own situation. As we shall see, the Philistines foreshadow today's adversary. Samson holds a special fascination because he was a lifelong Nazirite.

Who were the Philistines?

The Holy Spirit tells us that the Philistines were originally from Egypt (Gen. 10:13-14; see the appendix for comments on other views). They had been in the land before Abraham, many centuries before. To a landless traveler, they proved better neighbors than most. Abraham stayed in the land of the Philistines many days (Gen. 21:34). He even made a covenant with them (v. 32).

Here is the first strange thing: we would expect them to speak Egyptian, or an adaptation of that language. But it seems that they spoke Hebrew, the language of Israel! No one knows why this was. Whereas an Israelite would need an interpreter to speak to an Egyptian (Gen. 42:23), there was no language barrier with the Philistines. Even the names of their gods seem Hebrew. "Dagon," the Philistine fish-god, is a Hebrew word meaning "dear fish." This is very striking, because we Christians know that our own language retains words that show our origins. "Christ" is a Greek word (from the New Testament), and "Hallelujah" and "Amen" are Hebrew (from the Old Testament).

When Israel returned to the Promised Land, under Joshua, the Philistines were still there. But there had been some changes. Previously, they had lived under a king in the south of the land. Now they were ruled by the five lords of their five main cities. And they had moved. They now occupied lush country in the west, with harbors for ease of foreign trade.

There had been another change too: they had intermarried with giants. Who were these giants? They go by different names in Scripture. They were very large and cruel. Although of terrifying stature, they had been in retreat for some time (Deut. 2:20-23). But they found one safe haven—Philistia (Josh 11:22). Intermarriage produced Philistine giants. Goliath was 6 cubits and a span (1 Sam. 17:4)—between 9 1/2 and 11 1/2 feet tall!

Joshua overcame the Philistines, along with the other inhabitants of the land. To possess and keep the Promised Land, Israel had to remain faithful. It didn't. "The children of Israel again did evil in the sight of the Lord, and served the Baals" (Judg. 10:6). As a result (v. 7), "the anger of the Lord was hot against Israel; and He sold them into the hands of the Philistines and into the hands of the people of Ammon."

The Ammonites attacked the eastern part of the land. There, "the children of Israel cried out to the Lord" (Jud. 10:10), concerning their captivity. They refused to accept defeat at the hands of the Ammonites, and God liked that. He answered their prayers in due course, and Jephthah the judge drove out the Ammonite invaders.

But things were different in the west. There the Philistine rule had been gentle. As long as Israel did not rebel, there was no harshness to endure; no enslavement, no cruel taxes, no deportation—none of the usual marks of the conqueror. There was one restriction: the Israelites couldn't carry weapons. "There was neither sword nor spear found in the hand of any of the people who were with Saul and Jonathan" (1 Sam. 13:22). Indeed—lest anyone manufacture their own weapons, "all the Israelites would go down to the Philistines to sharpen each man's plowshare, his mattock, his ax, and his sickle" (v. 20).

So, while eastern Israel fought off the iron fist of Ammon, in the west they accepted the velvet glove of the Philistines. They became passive and submissive to their conquerors. When Samson valiantly withstood them, he had no support from his people. Life under the Philistines wasn't so bad, but there was one dream they must forego—God's call to "possess the land."

Today's Philistines

Studying what the Holy Spirit says about the Philistines, I am struck with the parallel in our own day. We too have a human adversary, who keeps the Kingdom of God at bay.

I am referring to the humanists. Who are these "humanists"? Humanists believe that there is no higher god than man. God's throne, they believe, is vacant. Man steps up to claim the empty throne. This means that *I* decide my lifestyle, my values, my destiny. There is no God to obey, no heaven and hell, and no supernatural power to save us.

Now that humanism is dominant in the West, people live by it without thinking. They view life—money, jobs, pleasures, the future, the family, and so on—apart from God. They cannot see God over all of life, offering grace in all these areas. They ignore His blueprints for living.

Humanism is a faith, even though it doesn't have temples. It is a religion without a god. It is a system of beliefs and actions, which rivals Christianity at every step. Don't forget this. Humanists like to present themselves as surveying religions and worldviews from a neutral standpoint. They use scientific language to convey a sense of being objective. In reality, humanism is as much a matter of faith as any religion. A *truly* objective look at reality would lead anyone to believe in the true God (Rom. 1:20).

Here are some of the parallels with the Philistines:

1. They were once such good neighbors

Abraham little guessed that his friendly neighbors would one day conquer his descendants. Likewise, the humanists emerged within *Christian* countries. From the beginning, Christians rubbed shoulders with them as good neighbors. We never saw them as a different faith—as we did Muslims, for instance. For a Christian to apostatize into Islam would shock the community. But to apostatize to humanism didn't seem so dreadful.

Charles Darwin, for instance, was once a Christian, and studied for the ministry. "Disbelief crept over me," he later said, "at a very slow rate, but was at last complete."[1] His apostasy to humanism didn't trouble his nineteenth-century contemporaries. When he reintroduced the old pagan theory of evolution,[2] it didn't feel like a return to pagan ideas. Christian England at that time was thrilled with new scientific ideas, and Darwin seemed only to be suggesting a new one.

Darwin's "attitude was that of the tolerant unaggressive agnostic, sympathizing with and helping the social and charitable influences of the English church in his parish. He was evidently most unwilling that his opinions on religious matters should influence others."[3]

2. They spoke the right language

Having a common language helps us feel at home with each

other. "When Israel went out of Egypt," it was a relief to leave "a people of strange language" (Ps. 114:1). There was no such strangeness with the Philistines.

Similarly, the humanists speak our sort of language. In fact, the term "humanist" can mean "a generous, humane person." Ancient pagans were amazed when Christians cared for the poor and weak—even pagan poor and weak. They thought the church crazy. Not so the humanists: they believe in loving one's neighbor. When they stand up for minority groups, when they care for the poor and needy, when they uphold the rights of the weak—they speak our language.

3. They intermarried with giants
The (comparatively) gentle Philistines of Abraham's day took on a cruel strain. We shall see the Philistines burning Samson's wife alive. Something similar happened to humanism. Any faith that denies the true God leads to the Devil. Humanism is no exception. Cruel giants began to appear in the ranks of the humanists.

Hitler was a humanist. His Nazi faith held to no god, and sought to continue man's evolution into a higher (Aryan) form. Millions of German Jews and gypsies died at his command. The Communist dictators Stalin and Mao were humanists too. They denied God. For them evolution led to the "highest" form of society—Communism. They too murdered countless millions of their fellow countrymen.

Today's Western humanists reject such blatant cruelty. But they are not free of it. Although they believe in being humane, they are at least partly responsible for the deaths of billions of unborn babies. And the harsh miseries of AIDS stem from the tolerance of homosexual behavior and fornication. "The tender mercies of the wicked are cruel" (Prov. 12:10).

4. They make gentle rulers

The Philistines held Israel in a gentle grip. Israel was not pro-voked to rebellion. Humanists are the same. Clearly, they dom-inate Western countries. Whether we look at governments, schools, the media or the "caring professions"—we see the same. It isn't the fear of the Lord, or the knowledge of His will that directs them. Their policies are predominantly humanistic.

But they use the velvet glove with Christians. They allow charitable status to our churches, and fund our voluntary pro-grams. We are a "voice in the community."

But, just as the Israelites were denied access to iron weapons, so are we. Today the main weapons for shaping public thought are the media and education. Christianity is pushed to the fringe in both of these. People in the West become commit-ted humanists without having weighed the rival claims. They drink in humanism with every school lesson, every television program, every newspaper article—and they don't realize what is going on. They repeat the orthodox beliefs of humanism without knowing why they believe them.

If Islam ruled the West, we Christians would be storming heaven with prayers for deliverance. But we rest easier under humanism, as Israel did in Samson's day.

5. Have we forgotten the Promised Land?

For Israel, submission under the Philistines meant renouncing the call to possess the land. They concentrated on their own internal affairs, and let the Philistines be. But we too have a "promised land"—we are to "make disciples of all the nations . . . teaching them to observe all things that I have commanded you" (Matt. 28:19-20). That includes this country, its government, schools, and so on.

Submissive Israel became spiritually mediocre, as Samson found when he needed help. What about us? At one time,

Christianity dominated the West. However imperfect those times were, they remain a challenge to us today.

Have we let our internal affairs dominate us? Have Christians with "the wrong views" become the enemy for us? Are we confronting our neighbors with Christ? Or have the humanists convinced us not to be "intolerant" or "fanatical" about religion?

Indeed, are *we* free from an insidious humanism? Theological liberals gained notoriety by importing humanistic notions: Jesus wasn't God incarnate, miracles didn't happen; the Bible isn't God's Word, homosexual behavior is acceptable. Church leaders declare these views, and we listen appalled.

But then we hear reports of shockingly slight knowledge of the Bible among believers. Without the light of the Word, we shall all be humanists, whether we know it or not.

Humanism in our sights

As we follow Samson's life, we will see that he was different from the rest. He did not accept Philistine rule. He was wide awake, while all slept. We shall relate this to the church in the West, and our struggle under humanism. Of course, physical violence is no part of our calling, but there is a spiritual battle to be fought—and that is no less demanding.

We shall learn more of humanism as we go along.[4] Meanwhile, the New Age movement is an emerging adversary. But in a sense, it also is humanistic. New Age thinkers look to a god-in-me to guide them. They know of no objective revelation of God, so it boils down to "what my god-in-me thinks." In practice this is the same as "what *I* think."[5]

Samson's special childhood

We are told two things about Samson's childhood: that the Lord blessed him as he grew (Jud. 13:24), and that he was a lifelong Nazirite (v. 7).

The first blessing was godly parents. Judges 13 paints a picture of a team, a man and wife with a shared faith. She submitted happily to her husband's headship; he took his responsibilities seriously and listened to her wisdom. We can see why God chose them: they were quick to obey, eager to worship, and full of faith.

Their child would "begin to deliver Israel out of the hand of the Philistines" (v. 5).

The Lord blessed him. "Blessing" in the Bible means both physical and spiritual good. God was preparing His chosen hero.

Then, in early manhood, we are told that "the Spirit of the Lord began to move upon him at Mahaneh Dan between Zorah and Eshtaol" (Jud. 13:25). The place "Mahaneh Dan" ("Camp of Dan") has special significance. It makes Samson's early life run parallel with Gideon's.

Gideon became a great war leader in God's power, but first he had to destroy the idols at home (Jud. 6:25ff). He seems to have found this harder than the great battles he later fought! This is understandable as once we have defeated the enemy within, we are fitted to beat him anywhere.

Samson was from the tribe of Dan. Much earlier (but recorded later in Judges—chapter 18) they had given up trying to possess their allotted territory. They made a central camp at Mahaneh Dan, and from there set out to find easily conquered territory outside the Promised Land. It was an act of cowardice and unbelief, and it didn't end there.

The city they captured was called Dan, and it became a center of idolatry, with its own graven image and false priesthood. This idolatry continued "all the time that the house of God was in Shiloh" (Jud. 18:31), until the "captivity of the land" (v. 30). It ended therefore around the same time that Samson is said to be moved by the Spirit at Mahaneh Dan. We note that Samson never went out of the promised land, but stayed in his tribe's proper territory, even in death (Jud. 16:31).

The ark of the covenant was captured and then returned to Israel, as we shall see. It was kept at Kiriath Jearim for the twenty years of Samson's ministry (1 Sam. 7:1-2). This Kiriath Jearim is near Mahaneh Dan (Jud. 18:12), Samson's base.

Where is this leading us? Samson is moved by the Spirit at the same time as his tribe give up their idolatrous center in Dan. The ark—the true center of worship—is moved to where Samson lives. From this, I strongly suspect that the Spirit had moved Samson to oppose his tribe's idolatry. He is rewarded by having the ark settled near his home base.

If this is so, then the Spirit did to Samson what he had done to Gideon. He led him first to oppose the enemy within—the idolatry of his own tribe. Then he could fight the battles against the pagans.

"The time has come for judgment to begin at the house of God," says the apostle, "and if it begins with us first, what will be the end of those who do not obey the gospel of God?" (1 Peter 4:17). Whether in judgment or mercy, God starts with His own people. When we pray about the evils in our humanistic land, we should be asking God for light, to see if such evils have infiltrated us too.

If we are offering ourselves to serve God, we must not be surprised if He sends us first to destroy the idols at home. Greed, selfishness, unbelief—these and many others must go.

The Nazirites

What did it mean for Samson to be a "Nazirite"? The Nazirite vow is described in Numbers 6. It was a special and unique sacrifice.

Some Old Covenant sacrifices relate to human sin, and were compulsory. They point to Jesus' death for us, which is essential for our salvation. Other sacrifices were not compulsory. The peace offerings, for instance, were voluntary. They gave the believer an opportunity to say a special "thank You, I love You" to God. The New Covenant equivalent to that is the "sacrifice of praise" (Heb. 13:15).

The Nazirite vow would normally last for years, and it expressed a special love and devotion toward God.

Samson was a lifelong Nazirite. This was almost unique: the only others were John the Baptist and Samuel.

Samuel and Samson were contemporaries (see the appendix). Like John the Baptist, they were born of hitherto barren women. Why two lifelong Nazirites at the same time?

Israel had compromised and submitted to the gentle rule of the Philistines. Only those who were different—not part of the crowd—could lead the counter attack. As we shall see, the Nazirite vow was a public and visible sacrifice to God. It singled you out from others; it made you different. These Nazirites were not compromised; God could use them.

It isn't easy for us to be different from the humanists around us. They don't seem alien; they vote as we do; listen to the same music, and laugh at the same jokes. Humanistic friends share our outrage at some injustice we have suffered. They have similar problems with their children. That's why it can seem so hard to bring up the subject of Christ and the Gospel. It's as if it were an intrusion; that it would create division where there is harmony.

Christians under persecution pray for us in the West. They see us with the clarity of their own situation. They suffer for Christ, and thus share His joy. They think us compromised by the insidious creeping death of humanism. They believe we need their clarity, their joy.

Yes, we must be different. We shall look at the Nazirite vow, and see what help it can give us today.

1. Nazirites did not cut their hair

"Does not even nature itself teach you," the Holy Spirit says, "that if a man has long hair, it is a dishonor to him?" (1 Cor. 11:14). In Bible times they knew this, so only a rebel (such as Absalom in 2 Sam. 14:26) would grow his hair long.

So don't think of the Nazirite as making a fashion statement! He looked wrong, and he knew it.

It was a sacrifice.

The hair is the only part of the body that can be harvested and sacrificed to God. It signified the whole body offered as a living sacrifice in complete commitment. The longer you endured your long hair, the more valuable it was as a sacrifice.

The Nazirite surrendered himself completely to God. We should all do that, but he did something more: he made it public. And he didn't mind looking foolish in the process.

When I was in school, I was offered an opportunity to represent my school in sports. My excitement was tempered by the fact that school practices and games were on Sundays. So I turned down the chance.

At times, I wondered if I had been foolish to do so. At that time I went to what I still think was the most boring church in the universe. I had given up playing sports for this?

I am so grateful now that God helped me to make the sacrifice. It was a public way to declare that He is my everything. And I found that if you go to church for Jesus, He will meet you, however dull the service is. When I hear people say that they weren't at church because it's boring, I thank God for teaching me that lesson early on.

Ask God how you can make public your absolute surrender to Him. Whatever the sacrifice costs, you will never regret it. "I am your shield," says the Lord, "your exceedingly great reward" (Gen. 15:1).

2. Nazirites refused grapes

Grapes and raisins were the tasty tidbits of those days; wine the finest drink. They represented God-given pleasures (Ps. 104:15).

In those days of close community, the feast was a central event. All through the feast, the Nazirite would have to refuse the innocent pleasures others enjoyed. His sacrifice was public.

Why give up enjoyable things? Because, if I am 100 percent for Jesus, I will have to give up some innocent pleasures. There is no sin in enjoying a warm bed in the morning. But to pray will mean making sacrifices: "With my soul I have desired You in the night," says the prophet. "Yes, by my spirit within me I will seek You early" (Isa. 26:9).

Jesus is our pattern. "In the morning, having risen a long while before daylight, He went out and departed to a solitary place; and there He prayed" (Mark 1:35).

I am so grateful that from the moment of my conversion, I was taught to seek God daily in prayer. I tried to get up early, and often failed to do so. But I knew I should, even when it became unfashionable to do so.

Part of the battle was to get to bed early the previous night. This would mean leaving a party when it would be fun to stay. It usually meant saying why you had to leave. Again, it made the inner commitment public. I think many people pitied me, but at least they realized that Jesus was more important to me than everything else.

3. Nazirites didn't go to funerals

In those days families were very close. This intimacy gave a wonderful sense of security and identity. The family educated, directed, financed, and protected you. The crucial family gathering was the funeral. Even estranged brothers like Jacob and Esau were united at their father's funeral (Gen. 35:29).

The Nazirite publicly sacrificed earthly security.

Jesus said: "He who loves father or mother more than Me is not worthy of Me. And he who loves son or daughter more than Me is not worthy of Me" (Matt. 10:37). To the would-be disciple who said "Lord, let me first go and bury my father," Jesus commanded: "Follow Me, and let the dead bury their own dead" (Matt. 8:21-22).

This is a wonderful world, and it is tempting to make ourselves entirely at home here. The heroes of faith sought a homeland (Heb. 11:14), but not here on earth. "They desire a better, that is, a heavenly country" (v. 16).

Really to walk by faith means walking on water. Sometimes there is nothing supporting us except the everlasting arms. However terrifying such times are, the resulting joy makes it all worthwhile.

When I lived in Guernsey, God called me to leave my settled ministry (and the house that went with it) and start something new. This was a terrifying prospect, because the family would then be homeless. Guernsey law prohibited foreigners from buying or renting houses in the normal way, unless they were granted a license.

I assumed God would get me a license, but when that didn't happen, it seemed that I would have to return to England. That would be a disaster; I had nowhere to go, nowhere to live. My only hope was an "open market" house, but these were far too expensive even to consider.

For the next several months, faith alternated with panic. The miracle happened at the last possible moment. God supplied the money for an "open market" house. The process involved coincidences, chance events, and downright miracles.

The full story is fun to tell, but it was dreadful living through it. I have vivid memories of awful fear, and my stomach twisted in a knot. I would seek God in desperation, and find a wonderful peace; but the fear always came back.

But the end result was a public witness to God that His will is worth more than earthly security.

On the threshold of greatness

We leave Samson as we first meet him: on the brink of great things. He is different. Not for him the mediocrity of a subdued Israel.

He is ready to make a difference.

Godly parents and his own sacrificial commitment have shaped him. The Spirit has begun to move him, and he has perhaps already confronted the idolatry of his own tribe.

He will not be pressed into a mold by the Philistines. He has broken the mold in his own life. Soon he will begin to break the molders. He will look to other Israelites to rise to the challenge.

He leaves us with the same challenge. Will we rise to the same sacrificial commitment? Will we make our Christianity public? Will we follow Christ rather than humanism in every area of our lives?

---

1. *Encyclopedia Britannica*, vol. 7, 843, © 1910.
2. To see how pagans have believed in evolution through the centuries, see Dr. Henry Morris' *The Long War Against God* (Baker Book House, 1989). It is becoming harder and harder for humanists to ignore the sheer weight of scientific evidence against evolution—see Richard Milton, *The Facts of Life* (Fourth Estate, 1992).
3. Ibid.
4. For those who want a thorough overview of humanism and what it believes, I recommend David Noebel, *Understanding the Times* (Summit Press, 1991).
5. For the humanistic basis of the New Age Movement, see Dr. Gary North's *Unholy Spirits* (Dominion Press, 1986).
6. See the appendix. Even if we agree to accept the traditional chronology, the exact sequence of events cannot be determined. I am making my own choices among the different options throughout this book. At that time, the eastern part of Israel was delivered from the Ammonites (Jud. 11). The western part, perhaps encouraged by the success in the east, tried to overcome the Philistines, and failed. This could be called "the captivity of the land," because the ark of the covenant was taken by the Philistines in the battle. "The glory has departed from Israel, for the ark of God has been captured" (1 Sam. 4:22).

FIRST STRENGTH

3

Judges 14:1-6

The Israelites walked with heads bowed, but Samson was different; not for him the despondency that gripped the nation. When the lion came, it found a man who expected to win.

Why were their heads bowed? It wasn't the sorrow that comes with repentance, although it should have been.

This is what had happened.

Ichabod—the glory departed

Fired no doubt by Israelite victory in the east (Jud. 11), western Israel decided to rise against their mild masters. They met the Philistines in battle (1 Sam. 4:1; see the appendix for explanations of the chronology). The Philistines won. Although mild in government, they were mighty in battle. Was that why God's people had lost? What could they do to ensure victory?

Eastern Israel had known the answer to that question. God had handed them over to the enemy, because of their sin. Prior to victory, eastern Israel had repented. "We have sinned!" they cried (Jud. 10:15). Then they got rid of their idols (v. 16).

Western Israel had not bowed their heads in penitence. Their victory came twenty years later, after they had finally repented (1 Sam. 7:3-4).

Meanwhile, lacking true repentance, they tried to win using religion. They decided to take the ark of the covenant with them. Surely this sacred object, which represented God's actual presence, would ensure victory! Israelite confidence knew no bounds, "and when the ark of the covenant of the Lord came into the camp, all Israel shouted so loudly that the earth shook" (1 Sam. 4:5).

Alas, without true repentance, such gestures were meaningless. Israel was defeated again, with heavier casualties. Worse still, the ark was captured.

When he heard this, old Eli died. Eli had judged Israel for forty years, but his weakness had cost Israel dearly. His sons, engaged in the holiest duties of Israel, were wicked men. Eli had failed to discipline them (1 Sam. 3:13), and so they died with 30,000 of the army, when the ark was captured.

As Eli died, his grandson was born. This child was named Ichabod—meaning "No Glory"—because the sacred ark was gone (1 Sam. 4:21). This was an all-time low for Israel. We can imagine them walking with heads bowed. But, sadly, their heads hung low because of defeat—not because of holy repentance.

Defeat always lowers morale—but it was specially true in this case. Their expectations had been built up upon a false hope. They had hoped that the Ark, which represented God's presence, would guarantee victory. But where was God's real presence? "I dwell in the high and holy place," says the Lord, "with him who has a contrite [broken, repentant] and humble spirit" (Isa. 57:15).

What is the lesson from this? It is that the Devil is quite happy for churches to become confident, provided that it is a false confidence. Had Israel repented after the loss of the ark,

Satan's scheme would have misfired. But it didn't; perhaps Israel fabricated a phony explanation for her defeat. Perhaps the leaders felt that they needed to save face.

The Devil knows that people remember these disappointments, however much they are covered over with excuses and plausible explanations. After a while, such people refuse to entertain any new hope. They have been disappointed too often. Then, when a true hope is raised—based on Jesus' supreme lordship—they cannot find any enthusiasm.

So we see Israel demoralized beneath a crushing defeat. At this point in history Samson began his life's work.

The two Nazirites

"What," you may ask, "was Samuel up to while all this was happening?" According to the traditional chronology, Samuel and Samson were born around the same time. They could not have been more different, nor more alike. As we have seen, they were both Nazirites. Even their names are similar, starting (in both Hebrew and English) with the same syllable. They had the same calling, too—both were judges.

Samson was a warrior, a man of physical courage and strength. He was a continual challenge to the Philistines. By contrast, Samuel was a quiet figure. He had a priestly function without—at that time—any political involvement. He was a prophet.

Samuel had the Word; Samson the power. Both worked miracles.

Taken together, they make up a David. "For our Gospel did not come to you in word only, but also in power" (1 Thess. 1:5). David was a prophet and a warrior. He ministered before the ark, and also led the armies. He was a man of action and a man of quiet contemplation.

The "super gun" strategy

Some years ago a Middle-Eastern country was banned from importing Western weapons. But they were very eager to have a "super gun"—a huge weapon that could fire over vast distances. To evade the ban, they came up with a novel strategy: to import the weapon in pieces. Parts of the gun's massive barrel came in as "piping," and its mechanism was "machinery." No single component appeared dangerous. Only with assembly would the danger be seen. The plan nearly worked.

God did the same with Samson and Samuel. On their own, neither posed a real threat, because neither was a leader. The Philistines soon learned that Israel wouldn't follow Samson, even after his great victory at Lehi.

This shouldn't surprise us; Samson was a loner. True leaders work with others. And Samson took appalling risks in battle—who would want to follow someone like that?

Samuel was no leader either. Even after his great victory, the people immediately asked for a king! The thought of being led by Samuel couldn't have been very appealing. He just wasn't the leader type.

Obviously, the Philistines would have been on the look-out for a potential leader among the Israelites. Had a David appeared, they would have snuffed him out while he was still young.

So, God produced two people who together made up one leader. He trained them both from infancy: they were Nazirites, and therefore different from the rest. Neither could have done without the other; together, they would set Israel free.

The Philistines watched Samson and Samuel grow. They little guessed that a "super gun" was being prepared to blast them out of the Promised Land!

Teamwork

As I write, I am involved in three areas of ministry. I am a church pastor, a Bible college principal, and a writer. In the church, I am one of two elders. Together we work with a group of leaders. We are a team, and I try to bring my distinctive contribution to it.

Even writing—which is such a solitary process—is teamwork for me. There is the wider vision of the publishers, and the insights of those who see early drafts of what I write.

I have learned that the church is a body—and each must play their part in it. The strength of the body lies in different parts working together.

Too often, churches establish their own emphasis and then try to "go it alone." Out of this comes inter-church rivalry. This is a terrible waste. There is no need to be frightened by the different emphases of other churches. On the contrary, it is our very differences that make our unity so powerful.

I believe that the churches are parts of a "super gun." God is waiting to assemble us. Our opponents have no idea what will happen when we are one! In Christ, we shall be unstoppable, and joy will erupt throughout our land.

A man's motives

We join Samson as he begins his adult life and its adventures. We find we must make a decision: how shall we interpret his actions? For some in the Bible, their inner motives are shown to us. We see David in action in 1 Samuel, and we can read his heart through the Psalms. Paul is busy in the Acts of the Apostles, and his intentions are revealed in his letters.

There is no such help with Samson. However, to make sense of any story, we *must* know the basic aims of the characters. For instance, if we heard that wicked men had evicted everyone from

God's temple, we would know that they had done wrong. Their wicked motives explain their action. Then we learn that *Jesus* evicted everyone from the temple. Jesus' aims were always entirely good. Thus, we know we must interpret his actions accordingly.

When I began this book, I already shared the modern view of Samson. That is, I saw him as an ungodly man, whom the Spirit occasionally anointed. The miracle was that God could further His purposes through this unfit instrument.

Then I realized that I must submit to the Spirit's only word about Samson outside the narrative of Judges—Hebrews 11:32-34. There I found him listed among the heroes of faith.

Nowadays, when some Christians talk about great faith, they are talking about miracles and answered prayer. Such a view of faith allows us to keep our low view of Samson, and then add: "And he had miraculous strength." The trouble is, this doesn't fit God's view of faith. For God, faith is primarily linked with godliness. This is the testimony of the Scriptures.

Might someone have faith for miracles, and still be ungodly? Yes, it is possible. But such a person would be "nothing": "Though I have all faith, so that I could remove mountains," says the apostle, "but have not love, I am nothing" (1 Cor. 13:2). The loveless are lawless (Rom. 13:10). To lawless miracle workers, Christ says: "I never knew you" (Matt. 7:21-23). God doesn't list lawless nothings—whom He doesn't know—in His list of heroes.

What matters is "faith working through love" (Gal. 5:6; see also 2 Peter 1:5-7). If faith doesn't produce loving godliness in action, it isn't real. "Faith without works is dead" (James 2:20). God's heroes of faith have living faith.

Samson's living faith

The reason is this: *God wants man to be righteous.* This is the vital thing. To work miracles, or to have mighty prayers answered is good, but it is not vital for salvation. But man by nature is unrighteous, "dead in trespasses and sins" (Eph. 2:1-3). Those whom God saves are given righteousness in two ways:

1. We are justified; that is, we are reckoned by God as righteous. This happens because Jesus takes and pays for our sin, and He gives us His righteous standing (see Rom. 3:21–4:25). We are instantly and entirely justified on conversion.

2. We are sanctified; that is, progressively made righteous in action. Our thoughts and actions become increasingly good and Christlike (see Rom. 6:1–8:27). Although this sanctification is always growing (2 Cor. 3:18), it is distinctly present at conversion. The true Christian simply doesn't go on committing serious sins (1 Cor. 6:9-11; Heb. 10:26–31; 1 John 3:4-10).

Although we can separate these two things—justification and sanctification—in our minds, they always occur together. "The grace of God that brings salvation has appeared to all men, teaching us that, denying ungodliness and worldly lusts, we should live soberly, righteously, and godly in the present age ... zealous for good works" (Titus 2:11-14).

It is the same grace which justifies us—"the kindness and the love of God our Savior toward man ... not by works of righteousness which we have done, but according to His mercy He saved us, through the washing of regeneration and renewing of the Holy Spirit, whom He poured out on us abundantly through Jesus Christ our Savior" (Titus 3:4-6).

This two-sided righteousness comes to every true believer. We receive it through faith: "By grace you have been saved, through faith" (Eph. 2:8). It must be through faith! How else could those who are dead in sin become righteous?

By faith we continue to believe we are justified; by faith we grow in active righteousness.

A hero of faith must be especially righteous. How could he

fail to be? Even if he worked no miracles, he must have right-eousness in heroic proportions.

Heroes of faith

This is what we see when we look through the list of heroes in Hebrews 11. Several of these heroes worked no miracles that we know of. It is their righteousness that the Spirit is emphasizing.

Look through the list:

• Abel, the first hero, "obtained witness that he was right-eous" (v. 4).

• Then Enoch diligently sought Him (v. 6).

• Noah "became heir of the righteousness which is accord-ing to faith" (v. 7).

And so the list continues. What does God say of Moses? Moses was the most powerful miracle worker of the Old Testament. His mighty prayers brought Egypt to economic and political ruin. We would expect his faith to be celebrated in a list of miracles. Instead we are told:

> Moses . . . refused to be called the son of Pharaoh's daughter, choosing rather to suffer affliction with the people of God than to enjoy the passing plea-sures of sin, esteeming the reproach of Christ greater riches than the treasures in Egypt; for he looked to the reward (vv. 24–26).

His faith led to obedience, willingness to suffer with Christ, refusal of sin. His faith led to righteousness.

When we get to Samson's section, where he is listed with other heroes, we do find mention of miraculous actions: they "subdued kingdoms . . . stopped the mouths of lions . . . quenched the violence of fire, escaped the edge of the sword . . . women received their dead raised to life again" (vv. 32-35). But the vital element is not missing: they "worked righteousness" (v. 33).

When I thought of all this, I realized that I could not think of Samson as an unrighteous man. I could not restrict his faith to miracles. I had to see his faith as God sees it—not that of a "nothing" whom Jesus never knew; nor a "dead" faith. I had to see him as sanctified by faith—heroically so.

Does that mean that he never sinned? Certainly not. Other heroes of faith sinned—Noah became drunk and vulnerable to sin, David committed adultery. But like Samson, their sins were not the whole story, and their lives were generally characterized by the righteousness of faith.

As my studies progressed, I found that I was not alone in wishing to see Samson in terms of Hebrews 11. Many have done so, especially the grand masters of the Word from the greatest era of English theology (see the appendix for mention of great books on Samson).

So, what of Samson's motives? Led by the Spirit in Hebrews 11, we shall read his exploits as motivated by the righteousness of faith. We shall see that apparently unspiritual actions are vindicated now that we know Samson's primary motives. Where Samson disobeyed God's Word, as in the matter with the prostitute, we shall learn about how a righteous man may lapse.

Whatever the other lessons, this we must learn: *the secret of strength is based on the righteousness of faith.* Do you hunger and thirst for righteousness? Until you do, you will never know the secret of strength.

Why a Philistine woman?
For some, the choice of a Philistine simply illustrates Samson's weakness. It is Samson "displaying a fatal weakness for Philistine women" according to one commentator.[1]

What are this commentator's presuppositions? He sees Samson as "undisciplined and immoral, his credentials as a man of God were few" since he "gave free rein to his appetites."[2]

I much prefer the view of Matthew Henry, for whom the testimony of the Spirit in Hebrews 11 is decisive. He says, concerning this marriage, "God put it into Samson's heart to make this choice, that he 'might have occasion against the Philistine.'"[3]

Can we answer the charge against Samson? Are his actions compatible with the righteousness of faith? We shall see.

1. Didn't God forbid intermarriage with the Philistines?

God forbade intermarriage with pagans (Deut. 7:3). But the primary reference was to the Canaanite tribes—peoples so wicked that God commanded their complete extinction! The Philistines weren't Canaanites; nor were they under sentence of total destruction.

What of the spirit of the Law? It was given to save the godly from compromise with the wicked (Deut. 7:4). Samson, however, never compromised with pagans. His marriage led to war against the pagans.

God did a similar thing with Hosea the prophet, whom he commanded to marry an immoral woman. Rather than becoming immoral himself, the prophet learned a lesson about immorality. His prophecy confronts Israel's immorality—spiritual and otherwise.

2. Why was this marriage "of the Lord"?

The marriage was "of the Lord; that he was seeking an occasion to move against the Philistines" (Jud. 14:4). Israel was too demoralized to stand against the Philistines. They were too fearful to let Samson lead them against their conquerors (Jud. 15:11). So God led Samson close to the Philistines, through the marriage, so that he could provoke a private quarrel.

Because it was a private matter, the Philistines could only respond against Samson—Israel remained uninvolved. Israel watched Samson's one-man war as mere spectators. Would his matchless valor ever awaken them?

3. What of Samson's parents' disapproval of the marriage?
Samson's "father and mother did not know that it [the marriage] was of the Lord" (Jud. 14:4). But they changed their minds and played their part in the wedding (v. 10).

Nowadays, parents normally have little part in the choice of their children's spouses. It was not so among the godly in Bible times (see for instance, 1 Cor. 7:36-38). If they didn't approve of a marriage, parents need not acquiesce in it.

We know, from Judges 13, that Samson's parents were fine, godly folk. Why did they change their minds about the marriage? Presumably someone informed them of God's will. Who told them? Remember, it was only Samson's parents who "did not know that it was of the Lord." Presumably Samson, who knew the "moving of the Spirit" (Jud. 13:25), was aware of God's will in the matter. No doubt he told his parents; hence their support for this strange match.

There is no reason to doubt Samson's righteousness in the matter of the marriage. Not that we should imitate Samson in this respect: his was an unusual path. We follow him as he goes into the lions' den of Philistine society, and wait to see how he will fare.

Before he gets there, he is in for a surprise.

The moment
Samson is traveling with his parents to Timnah to initiate the wedding arrangements. They come to the vineyards of Timnah (Jud. 14:5).

What is the significance of the vineyard? Our unfriendly commentator says that "the mention of the vineyard in v. 5 may mean that Samson broke another Nazirite law by eating some grapes."[4]

There is not the least suggestion anywhere that this was so.

But this illustrates an important point. One barrier to our oneness in Christ is unfounded suspicion. Our unfriendly commentator can assume the worst about Samson—contrary to the Spirit's testimony (Heb. 11:32–34).

Might we also harbor unfair suspicions about one another? Obviously we must protect the church from heresy. But we accept caricatures of fellow believers all too easily. One of our strengths is the wonderful variety of our styles and cultures. But instead of rejoicing in this diversity we become suspicious of others' strangeness. "It's a dead church," we say. Or, "They're not really very biblical." Do we really know that this is so?

The Bible shows us how to recognize heresy and hypocrisy. But what does the Spirit say of believers? However weak we may be, we are God's temple, His beloved people.

If we accept the testimony of the Spirit, we will accept fellow believers as brothers. We will not easily believe ill of one another. We will not judge each other, for "who are you to judge another's servant? To his own master he stands or falls. Indeed, he will be made to stand, for God is able to make him stand" (Rom. 14:4).

So what of the vineyard? Why does the Scripture mention it? A vineyard was the last place you would expect to find a lion. Why? Because lions eat wild animals, and wild animals stay away from places humans frequent. I suspect that this lion had developed a taste for people—it came where people (and not animals) would be found. If that is so, then Samson is faced with a predator who knows the ways of men, and how to catch its prey.

Alone he walks, scarcely aware of what is around him. He is

in a cultivated land, and may meet a vinedresser, but he doesn't care. In any case, there is no sound—he is clearly quite alone.

His feet follow the path without thought; his mind is taken up with other things, when suddenly he sees a flash of golden mane! There is a flurry of claws and ravening teeth! A moment to turn—dodge—flee for his life!

The great cat is used to such maneuvers. A lifetime predator, it knows every trick of the chase. Its startled victims will move with desperate speed; will duck, side step—anything to elude capture. But the lion, which is "mighty among beasts and does not turn away from any" (Prov. 30:30) is master of all these strategies.

Samson, rudely awoken from his reveries, has one moment—and only one—in which to react. He does not hesitate. "He tore the lion apart as one would have torn apart a young goat, though he had nothing in his hand" (Jud. 14:6).

In that brief moment, "the Spirit of the Lord came mightily upon him" and the predator became the prey.

The moment passes. There at his feet, lies the mightiest of beasts. As for Samson, he is not even marked, so that when his parents see him shortly after, there is no sign of what has happened.

Normally, several brave men, well armed, would set out to kill a lion. But Samson had nothing in his hands. He wasn't ready, he had no plan. Suddenly the danger was there and the Spirit was upon him. He still felt the excitement of the Spirit's anointing and his newfound miraculous strength.

Let's examine what happened. Only a fool will attack a lion without a weapon. A sane man will try to escape. It doesn't appear that Samson did this. Why did he attack? "The Spirit of the Lord came mightily upon him" (Jud. 14:6). What does that mean? And how did he know that it really was the Spirit? After all, we all feel things. Sometimes we have thought God was leading us, but events have proved we were mistaken. On the other hand, we can dismiss as mere imagination what turns out to have been God's prompting.

There are ways of testing these strong impressions. But Samson had no time; he had to react instantly. He attacked the lion in faith that he had been anointed with miraculous strength. His faith must have been very strong. The urge to flee an attacking lion would be well-nigh irresistible.

This is something we need to examine in detail. After all, it was thus that Samson found part of the secret of strength. We too need God's power if we are to serve Christ in our day. We need to learn what Samson learned.

There are two things to look at: how we know what is truly of the Spirit; and how to respond when He moves us.

1. Recognizing the Spirit's leading

Samson experienced a powerful inner impression; an intuitive feeling. It told him that he had been given supernatural strength. He had either to believe it and fight—or disbelieve and run. With only a moment in which to decide, Samson needed to know God's voice. How did he do that?

There is only one answer: he knew the Word of God. It is clear that Samson was familiar with the Bible, so far as it had been written. We know this, because he was soon in the ministry of a judge (Jud. 15:20). We shall see that this required an intimate knowledge of the Word.

The Bible is God speaking through inspired men. It is infallibly God's Word, every "jot and tittle." Whatever inner impressions we get from God must harmonize with the infallible Word and share its character and aims. If they don't, then it is these inner impressions which are wrong.

As we read the Bible, we are hearing directly from God. As we read it prayerfully, we sense the inner voice of the Spirit, Who confirms the Word. A familiarity with the Bible will give us the vital "feel" for God's authentic voice.

We will never acquire this familiarity, and grow in it, without self-discipline. We know that Samson knew how to be disciplined for God—he was a Nazirite.

2. Learning God's ways by experience
God will teach us to know Him through a disciplined and prayerful study of His Word. But when the moment comes, it is still rather scary to respond to the Spirit's guidance.

Samson had been "moved by the Spirit" already. He followed an extraordinary impulse, and found his faith rewarded.

The first time I felt led by the Spirit was when God called me to the ministry. The Bible teaches that only some are called to the full-time ministry (Acts 20:28; Col. 4:17). The only way to know if one is, is by a specific call. Churches recognize this, and have various ways to test the call.

This is normal within church life. But it is very strange when it happens to you! I felt utterly unsuitable for the ministry, but I discovered that only faith is needed. If God says, "Go," then faith should just go. God can use anyone.

God came upon Samson with the power to kill the lion. His power is available to us too but our calling is different. We are called to lead people to Christ. But the same supernatural power is needed.

Some years ago, I was asked to pray for a woman whose ankle had been badly broken in a car accident. She was unable to walk without crutches. Such a prayer calls for great confidence. At that time, I was immersed in the dilemmas of a spiritual battle, and not in the mood for prayers of confidence!

I invited the woman to sit, and knelt to pray. "What am I going to do?" I asked the Lord. Immediately, I felt a strong impression. "Ask if you may lay hands on her." It seemed to be the Spirit. I did so.

"What now?" I asked.

"Say: 'Be healed in Jesus' name.'"

I was too exhausted to think up anything more dramatic—so I just said it. "Now what?"

"Ask her to stand up."

I already knew that she couldn't stand without the crutches. I didn't want her falling down in agony and it being my fault! But neither did I want to disobey God. Were these impressions from God? I thought so.

I knew I couldn't hesitate—to delay would be the same as to disobey. So I asked her to stand. She was very surprised—it was the first time she had seen anyone pray for a miraculous healing. But she did stand. You should have seen her face when she found herself able to walk without pain, without the crutches! Come to think of it, you should have seen mine too!

I kept in touch with her long enough to learn the doctor's response. He was amazed at her changed condition; he found God's power quite inexplicable.

I tell this story to illustrate how difficult it is to follow these inner impulses in faith. I felt highly vulnerable as I did so! Afterward, I was so glad I had done it.

It's easy to see how an event of this nature helps. It demonstrates God's love for our whole being. It witnesses to God's power to all who see it. Who knows if that doctor thought more about Christ because of what he saw?

I have often seen God do things like this. In my experience, there is nearly always an inner lead from the Spirit, as well as the necessity for faith on my part. On another occasion, a girl asked us to pray for her back. Although the girl was part of our church youth group, I knew that she was being sexually immoral. An inner impulse told me that the bad back and the immorality were somehow connected.

But how could I broach the subject without betraying what I knew in confidence? I prayed, and I felt a name coming into my mind. It seemed that the Spirit was giving me this name. So I asked the girl whether the name meant anything to her. Again, I felt very vulnerable: what would I do if she said: "Who's he?"? Why not just pray for the back and avoid embarrassment?

Instead, she became very tearful. The name turned out to be that of the person (unknown to any of us) who had first led her into immorality. Realizing that God knew everything she was doing shocked her into repentance. She confessed her current immorality, and vowed to cease from it.

God did heal her back, but the repentance was the vital thing.

How about you?

These inner impressions aren't dramatic—although the results can be. I find that many Christians have them, but tend often to reject them as "just my imagination."

They aren't just for leaders, or only for church services.

There is a lovely park close to our house, and I sometimes take the children there. A few years ago, I was playing hide-and-seek with them, and couldn't find one of the girls. She is very good at not getting lost, but I began to grow worried.

"Where is she?" I asked. Fathers need help, and who better to ask than Father God? I felt an inner impression that she was all right. That was comforting. Then I felt an impression of where to walk to find her. This quiet impression led me among trees, past undergrowth, down paths. After a while I found that

I had been led directly to her! She was very well hidden, with her back to me. She was amazed that I had found her!

I had learned something new: God is with His people, even in ordinary life. He will lead us and help us.

You aren't Samson; you may not be in Christian ministry; perhaps you aren't a parent. But whoever you are, your Lord wants you to know Him through disciplined study of the Word. He wants you to recognize His guidance. He will lead you; He wants you to believe—and follow.

It is the secret of strength—or part of it, at least.

Some Christians feel unhappy about the miracles in today's church. They feel that it is sometimes associated with unsound doctrines. Is this true? It needn't be.[5]

Or perhaps they feel that Christian maturity is more important than these displays of power. It is, but why can't we have both? Both are there in the Bible.

We leave Samson with the lion at his feet. He has taken an important step. Now he knows that the Spirit leads him, and that he can trust that leading. The result is supernatural strength.

He is about to be joined to the Philistine community through marriage.

Light will join darkness, and there will be an explosion!

---

1. Herbert Wolf, "Judges" in *The Expositor's Bible Commentary*, vol. 3 (Zondervan, 1992), 465.
2. Ibid. 381.
3. Henry on Judges 14:4.
4. Wolf, 467.
5. To see present-day miracles explained in the context of sound, classically biblical theology, see Wayne Grudem's *Systematic Theology* (IVP, 1994), 1063 ff.

THE SPHINX THINKS 4

Judges 14:7-14

Samson and his parents returned to Timnah for the wedding. On the way, Samson went to look at the body of the lion he killed, and found a beehive there. The honey was a welcome surprise. They all enjoyed it, although Samson's parents had no idea where it came from.

Samson followed the local customs, and gave a week-long party to celebrate the wedding. He didn't seem to have had any friends to invite, or at least none who would join in a Philistine party. So the Philistines provided him with thirty companions.

A Philistine town; a Philistine house; Philistine people. They are celebrating the wedding of a Philistine girl. Philistine conversation; Philistine jokes; Philistine attitudes.

But wait—here's someone who doesn't fit! It's the Israelite, with his plaits of long hair and strange customs. He doesn't drink wine, or eat grapes. He doesn't laugh at all the Philistine jokes, nor agree with all their views.

Why do we keep looking at him? We are struck by something even stranger about him: he is so assured! The son of a conquered race, the odd-man-out on enemy territory—surely such a man would look sheepish? He would hide his disapproval of an alien culture. He would laugh when the others laughed—even if he suspected they were laughing at him!

Instead the Israelite is about to attack. He demands the attention of all. Our amazement increases—he is going to take them all on in a trial of wisdom! One against thirty doesn't faze him. The stakes are high enough that they cannot say no. Not that they want to; they are glad of a chance to take this cocky Israelite down a peg or two.

The Israelite poses his question. All around him brows knit in thought. Riddles are their territory—this uncultured Israelite cannot match their sophistication! But their thinking is getting them nowhere.

Suddenly, it is the conquerors who are at a disadvantage. One Israelite dominates them all. Their proud eyes drop before him. They will do anything to humiliate him!

Long hours and days pass as the Philistines try to crack the riddle. While they are thinking, we shall see how Samson fares in a different contest.

What about the body?

Some today accuse Samson of breaking his Nazirite vow when he took the honey out of the lion's carcass. "Heedless of the Nazirite vow," says our unfriendly commentator, "he scooped out some delicious honey."[1] This commentator doesn't even approve of Samson killing the lion: "Samson said nothing to his parents about his feat [of killing the lion] because his contact with the dead lion violated his Nazirite vow (cf. Num.6:6, 9)."[2]

Not only is Samson blamed for getting the honey—he

shouldn't have killed the lion in the first place! It seems that everything Samson does is wrong. Presumably he should have let the lion kill him!

Can Samson's actions be reconciled with the Spirit's testimony that he was a hero of faith? I believe so.

1. Nazirites avoided the bodies of dead people

The Nazirite "should not go near a dead body" (Num. 6:6). But the context is the deaths of the Nazarite's parents. In fact, the Hebrew for "dead body" here is literally "dead soul," an expression used only for people in the Bible—not animals. This same expression comes in Leviticus 21:11, "Nor shall he go near any dead body, nor defile himself for his father or his mother." The Nazirite must avoid the dead bodies of people. There is never a mention of Nazirites having to avoid dead animals.

2. Animal products?

Even if God had dead animals in mind, surely animal products were exempt. In those days, people's clothing and equipment were made from animal skins. Was a Nazirite forbidden to touch those? If so, then John the Baptist sinned by being "clothed with camel's hair and with a leather belt around his waist" (Mark 1:6). But Jesus honors John too highly for us to accuse him like this.

In any case, we should ask what state the carcass of the lion was in when Samson returned to it. Bees don't make hives in dead flesh. Anyway, dead meat is soon eaten by scavengers. But in that hot climate, carcasses can dry up like mummies without rotting. They become more like hollow trees (where bees like to have their hives).[3] In other words, the carcass was no more "dead flesh" than John the Baptist's clothes.

We deduce that no guilt is attached to Samson in all this.

Wisdom "in the sight of the peoples"

Why did Samson pose a riddle? Why were the Philistines interested in it? If we are to understand, we must take a step back and ask: "What was the relationship between Israel and the other nations in Old Testament times?"

God established His people as a distinct nation. They were to stay separate from the other nations, lest they learn evil ways by being too friendly. This separation lay behind the food laws, which stopped them from socializing with other nations. They mustn't learn from the pagans. But were the pagans to learn from them?

Yes, they were. That was the purpose of the separation. Observe them carefully, for this will show:

> your wisdom and your understanding in the sight of the peoples who will hear all these statutes, and say, "Surely this great nation is a wise and understanding people." For what great nation is there that has God so near to it, as the Lord our God is to us, for whatever reason we may call upon Him? And what great nation is there that has such statutes and righteous judgments as are in all this law which I set before you this day? (Deut. 4:6-8)

Israel was to impress the nations with its "wisdom." Wisdom in Scripture covers all areas of life: spiritual, intellectual, and practical. There were to be two impressive things about the nation. First, God would be seen "so near to it." This meant that God would answer the people's prayers, and this miraculous provision would be evident to outsiders.

Second, God's people have "statutes and righteous judgments," the wisdom of which are unmistakable. Pagans aren't necessarily impressed with the Bible way. But it works. Once God's ways are seen to work, their wisdom becomes evident.

The point is that all this would be "in the sight of the peoples." God wanted unbelievers to see His ways. We think of Old Testament Israel as being separated from the peoples so as not to be corrupted by them. And they were separate, but not that separate! They had a witness to make to the pagans concerning God's wisdom.

Israel had a "gospel" to offer. Anyone could repent of their idolatrous gods, and turn to the true God. Anyone could—and some did.

There was Ruth the Moabite; Uriah the Hittite; Rahab of Jericho. Rahab, listed among the heroes of faith (Heb. 11:31), is so striking! She was of the people of Jericho. That wicked city had been condemned to wholesale slaughter for its wickedness. No doubt Rahab was as wicked as any—she was a prostitute—until she came to faith.

Wherein did her heroic faith lie? Although a pagan, she came to believe that the "Lord [i.e., 'Jehovah,' the name for the true God] your God, He is God in heaven above and on earth beneath" (Josh. 2:11). She proved her faith genuine by saving the lives of the Israelite spies. How easily she was saved, when others—perhaps less wicked than she had been—were not! She saw the wisdom and grace of God in His people. She saw and believed.

Rahab joined Israel. Naaman didn't. He was commander of Syria's army, but he was a leper. An Israelite slave witnessed to God's power to heal through Elisha. Naaman went to Elisha, and was healed. That led him to faith in the true God. From now on, he would worship only the Lord (2 Kings 5:17). He didn't move to Israel, but took some Israelite soil, and worshiped the true God on it in his home country.

The revelation of the true God went much further afield than that. Amazingly, the Ten Commandments got to America around the twelfth century B.C. They are written in Hebrew on an eighty-ton boulder, near Las Lunas, New Mexico![4] Some Israelite must have gone to America—perhaps a trader—and taken the knowledge of the truth. I wonder how many twelfth-century B.C. American believers we shall meet in heaven.

Several centuries later, a whole city—Nineveh—"repented at the preaching of Jonah" (Matt. 12:41).

The call to witness

As far as we know, most of those who learned of Israel did not repent. Israel's infidelities were partly to blame for this. But the blindness of sinful man cannot be excused. So we shouldn't think of the witness of Old Testament Israel as a failure. Paul calls it "being led in triumph" when he was "a fragrance of his knowledge in every place." To the unbeliever, he became an "aroma of death"—but that didn't detract from the triumph. The main thing was that the Gospel was being preached in sincerity, without being watered down (2 Cor. 2:14-17).

God is glorified in His grace when the Rahabs believe and are saved. But He is glorified too when He judges those who refuse the truth (Ezek. 28:22). That's why several prophets had messages for the pagan nations (see Isa. 13–23; Jer. 46–51). These messages threatened punishment and implied that those nations ought to repent. They should have seen what was visible "in the sight of the peoples."

Solomon's was the most successful witness. "All the earth sought the presence of Solomon to hear his wisdom, which God had put in his heart" (1 Kings 10:24). What an amazing impact he had! One who came was the Queen of Sheba.

"Now when the queen of Sheba heard of the fame of

Solomon concerning the name of the Lord, she came to test him with hard questions" (1 Kings 10:1). She ended up very impressed with Solomon's wisdom and, therefore, with his God. "Blessed be the Lord your God," she exclaims (v. 9).

We are told that she examined Solomon's temple very closely, and may well have built a copy of it when she got home. I say this because Velikovsky identifies her with Hatsheput, an Egyptian queen. Velikovsky gives us her account of the trip to "God's Land," how impressed she was, and how she built a copy of Solomon's temple on her return.[5]

What have we learned? That Israel had wisdom to offer the pagans, which could lead to faith and salvation; that the queen tested this wisdom with hard questions.

This brings us back to Samson, because the Hebrew word used here for "hard questions" is "riddles"—the very word that Samson used. Now we have a clue as to why Samson asked the Philistines a riddle. It wasn't just a puzzle, it was a test of wisdom. "Riddles" appear in the same sense in the Book of Proverbs (Prov. 1:6).

Samson wanted to test their wisdom and offer a better one. He knew that he would "begin to deliver Israel out of the hand of the Philistines" (Jud. 13:5). So, before battle commenced, he made an offer of peace (the riddle)—as God's people must (see Deut. 20:10-11). Samson found, like the apostles, that his peace returned to him (see Matthew 10:13). But it had still been worth a try.

Samson's riddle

The Philistines originally came from Egypt. The Egyptians prided themselves on their ancient wisdom. One of their symbols of wisdom was the Sphinx—a mythological riddler. It had a lion's body (take note), with the head of a human. The biggest Sphinx is 189 feet long, near the Great Pyramid at Giza.

No doubt the Philistines felt that they had inherited the ancient wisdom of their Egyptian fathers. A contest of "wisdom skills"—such as Samson's riddle—would put them on home ground. They wouldn't expect an Israelite to beat them.

But Samson had beaten a lion on the way. He knew he could beat the lionlike Sphinx too.

This is the riddle:

> Out of the eater came something to eat,
> And out of the strong came something sweet (Jud. 14:14).

Remember, it isn't merely a puzzle. We expect it to contain hidden wisdom, a wisdom that would benefit the Philistines.

I tried to put myself in the Philistines' shoes, and see what they might have made of it. Obviously, they could not have known about Samson's experiences with the lion. So where would they have started?

My first stop was the Exodus. The Philistines would have been familiar with that great event. How could they not? It had brought devastation on the greatest nation of the day. Jehovah had certainly proved to be "strong" then! In fact, He had been an "eater," because He had consumed most of the crops and livestock of the country, in the plagues.

Had this strong eater given "something to eat"? Yes, He had fed His people with the miraculous manna. Strangely enough, this food was "sweet" like honey (Ex. 16:31).

So, I would have asked Samson whether the riddle pointed to the Exodus. He would have said "No." My next question would have been: "Is it something similar to the Exodus events?"

The answer to that would have had to have been "Yes." The

wisdom of the Exodus—that is, its theology-in-life meaning—
is this: God gives His people power to overcome the enemy, and
then He feeds them. The Egyptians who killed the Israelite
babies were like a savage lion. Israel was as powerless before
them as an unarmed man before a lion. But God had empowered Samson's muscles, just as He had Moses' staff. When
Samson found the honey, it seemed as much a miracle as the
manna.

We have the same miracle in our Gospel today. We, like
Samson, were powerless before the "roaring lion" which is Satan
(1 Peter 5:8). God showed fearsome strength to defeat that lion
for us. But now we are amazed at the sweetness of His grace to
us. His word is "sweeter also than honey and the honeycomb"
(Ps. 19:10).

I think the Philistines ought to have guessed that the "grace"
was the wisdom in the riddle. From that they could have
guessed their way to Samson's recent deliverance from the lion,
and God's special gift of honey. Or perhaps it would have been
too hard.

Either way, it would have been so good if the Philistines had
spent the seven days of the feast thinking about the grace of
God. After a while, they might have forgotten the prize—and
begun to desire something better. Why shouldn't they have
found what Rahab found?

How can we learn from Samson as he offers wisdom to the
Philistines? Surely we can have more confidence than he, because
we live in days when millions are turning to the true God.

Wise witnesses
Our message is wise—so too should be our method. "He who
wins souls is wise" (Prov. 11:30).

Why did Samson ask a riddle rather than deliver a sermon?

Clearly, the Philistines would never have listened to the sermon. At least the riddle made them think.

Had they confessed their failure to solve it, Samson would have told the story of the lion. That too would have made them think. It was a miracle story that could easily be verified, simply by examining the lion's body so fiercely torn apart. It spoke eloquently of God's love and power.

Let's see how we would apply this today:

1. Miracle stories

Walking with God is a matter of constant miracles. Nearly all of them are the little things—tax rebates in the nick of time; weather that clears up in time for the barbecue; exams passed unexpectedly. Although undramatic, these are the things that life is made of. Your neighbor recognizes something in these answered prayers; something he doesn't have.

Don't be shy to speak of them! They are a part of normal life—why keep them secret?

Humanism teaches people to explain away miracles. It seems that they will go to any lengths, however irrational, rather than believe a miracle! It is good, therefore, if the miracle happens to the unbeliever. It is a lot harder to reject your own experience!

Hence it is a good thing to pray for non-Christians. Churches nowadays sometimes deliver leaflets to the homes in their area, offering their prayers. "If you would like us to pray for you, just let us know," the leaflet says. The non-Christians state their need, but don't have to give their name or address. The church prays, and it is up to the unbeliever to draw his own conclusions when the prayer is answered.

Neighbors will often mention their needs: problems with children, illnesses, shortages of money. Why not offer to pray for them?

2. Riddles

Samson's riddle challenged the wisdom of the Philistines. He had a higher wisdom to offer, as do we.

How shall we offer the wisdom of God? It isn't easy, because our humanistic society thinks that rationality and objective understanding belong to them. In their minds, faith and rationality don't go together. "You have faith," they tell us. They mean that we don't have reason.

I think that some of us half believe them. We are forgetting the foundation our faith has in solid facts, and unbreakable logic. We offer Christ as "the One to answer your problem," which He definitely is. But we should also say that rational thought leads inevitably to Him—provided it stays objective.

If we had more confidence in the rational basis of our faith, we could challenge the "wisdom" of non-Christians. My experience is that many highly intelligent non-Christians have amazingly illogical views. They think that they are rational people in a scientific age. It turns out that they have a blind faith in the "there is no god" of humanism—and no evidence for it.

Let us look at the rational basis for our faith.

Design and the designer

Don't be surprised when I say that common sense sees God when it looks at the world. God Himself declares that the facts point only one way. If people can't see God in the Creation around them, it is because they don't *want* to. Their ignorance is *not* innocent. Look at what the Bible says:

> What may be known of God is manifest in them
> [i.e. unrighteous men], for God has shown it to
> them. For since the creation of the world His invis-
> ible attributes are clearly seen, being understood by

the things that are made, even His eternal power and Godhead, so that they are without excuse, because, although they knew God, they did not glorify Him as God, nor were thankful, but became futile in their thoughts, and their foolish hearts were darkened (Rom. 1:19-21).

You don't have to be a scientist, the evidence is unmistakable for the ordinary person: God is "known . . . shown . . . clearly seen . . . they knew." A universe patently designed must have a designer. But Creation demonstrates more than that. It is not only clear that God is—we can see *what* He is. "*What may be known* of God is manifest . . . His invisible attributes . . . even His eternal power and Godhead." What God has revealed specifically in the Bible is also there in Creation in shaded outline.

Before we go too far along this road, we should ask: "What use is it to the ordinary believer?"

It is highly useful—if we are to learn from Samson.

Riddles for the modern man

Common sense is compelling. We hate to abandon it. As G.K. Chesterton observed, humanistic beliefs tend to relinquish common sense as a first step. They have to, for how else could they believe in a designed universe without a designer? How else could they reduce the soul to mere electrical impulses in the brain?

It is the philosophers who have established the beliefs of humanism. Ordinary folk don't read their books, but do find themselves believing their beliefs. They don't realize that what they believe is contrary to common sense. So, an appeal to common sense threatens their whole faith. Of course, they don't know that. If only we could lead them to think consistently about the facts of life! Who knows if God might corner them and force them into everlasting joy?

That's why God comes to them with riddles.

The riddle of the source
God asks:

> Who has measured the waters in the hollow of
> His hand,
> Measured heaven with a span
> And calculated the dust of the earth in a measure?
> Weighed the mountains in scales
> And the hills in a balance? (Isa. 40:12)

The logic of the question is this: the source of everything must be greater than itself. A work of art (a thing) must come from an artist (a person). A person is greater than a thing. Logic tells us that a painting (a thing) cannot produce a painter (a person)!

If a ball breaks your window, something must have sent it. It may have been an explosion, or the force of gravity, or even your innocent-looking child, who is just hiding the baseball bat. The ball cannot have hit itself, whatever your child says.

So, God asks "Who is big enough to be the source of creation?" Whoever it is, He must be bigger than the universe—"waters . . . heaven [i.e., space] . . . the earth . . . the mountains." It must be a "who"—not a "what," because creation includes people who cannot have the impersonal as a source.

You and your neighbor are watching the beauty of a sunset. Or perhaps you are discussing a TV program about the vastness of space. "Where do you think it all came from?" you ask.

Your neighbor is a good humanist. "Evolution," he dutifully replies.

Then you ask your riddles. "Do really believe that impersonal matter and blind chance could produce the universe?" Maybe you begin to talk about yourselves, "fearfully and wonderfully made" (Ps. 139:14). Can the beauties of our soul—personality, love, creativity, artistry, rationality—can they come from such an inferior source?

Your neighbor's common sense rebels within him. He must now repress common sense, or begin to open his mind.

Sinful man does "suppress the truth in unrighteousness" (Rom. 1:18), but not always. Maybe the Holy Spirit begins to speak through common sense to him. The source of the universe, obviously, must be bigger than the universe. It cannot therefore be mere matter and luck. Can there really be a God? He begins to think the unthinkable.

The riddle of design
Here is another riddle from God:

> Does the hawk fly by your wisdom,
> And spread its wings toward the south? (Job 39:26)

The context of this riddle is God's series of questions to Job. Job is made to see the vastness and order of the universe—and how foolish it is to question God's government of it.

For our purposes, we should ask: "Whose *wisdom* designed our marvelous universe?" A designed universe must have had a designer; so common sense tells us. In the same way we know that computers do not emerge from some mindless cluster of chance events. Would a piece of leather evolve into a shoe—a shoe with a manmade sole, laces, and a rather trendy style?

The riddle takes it further than that. All hawks fly by a common design. In fact, all the universe (so far as we can examine it) bears the marks of a single designer. Gravity holds atoms together throughout the whole universe. Australia is governed by the same natural laws as Europe.

We are seeing the work of one designer—not several rival designers.

The riddle of goodness

> The Lord is good to all,
> And His tender mercies are over all His works
> (Ps. 145:9).

Common sense makes God's "invisible attributes" visible. Encourage your neighbor to look beyond the suffering and disasters of today's world. Yes, man's cruelty to man mars human life. Yes, there are earthquakes and volcanoes. But these are exceptional. What are the essential features of human life?

Mankind must eat, sleep, and reproduce. Without these things, the human race would die out. The need to survive would drive us to do these things anyway. "But do you enjoy them?" you ask.

Yes, your neighbor does. Show your neighbor the pleasure that has been put into our essential activities. Why is there such joy in these simple things of life? Why are love and friendship so wonderful (unless marred by sin)? Good sense would have driven mankind to operate in teamwork and cooperation—why was joy added to it?

Your neighbor can put two and two together. Common sense tells him that the Designer is good to all—even those who reject Him. God need not have been so good to us.

Of course, this raises the riddle of why is there suffering—which leads to issues of the Fall, judgment, and the righteous being perfected through suffering. But make sure your neighbor doesn't miss the most obvious fact of all—this world was designed by Someone who enjoyed making us happy.

The riddle of revelation

> God, who made the world and everything in it, since He is Lord of heaven and earth, does not dwell in temples made with hands. Nor is He worshiped with men's hands, as though He needed anything, since He gives to all life, breath, and all things. And He has made from one blood every nation of men to dwell on all the face of the earth, and has determined their preappointed times and the boundaries of their dwellings, so that they should seek the Lord, in the hope that they might grope for Him and find Him, though He is not far from each one of us (Acts 17:24-27).

"So that they should seek the Lord." Creation tells us something of God. Why? Obviously because He wishes to be known. But creation itself gives us only limited knowledge. It follows therefore that people should "seek the Lord, in the hope that they might grope for Him and find Him." There must be a more complete knowledge available.

If your neighbor has followed your riddles so far, he may be tempted to stop short. "Well, well," he says, "maybe there is a God." Or perhaps he is a New Ager, or a mystical type. Perhaps he already believes there is a God. Many people have their own private view of what God is like. They don't need to "seek God and find Him," because they already have their own ideas.

They need to hear a little common sense.

"If God reveals something of Himself in creation," you say, "it must be so that He might be known. But if the knowledge of God were only a matter of our inner perceptions and feelings, He would never be clearly known." Experience tells us that those whose inner perceptions guide them come to entirely different conclusions. "Don't you think that God could have found a way to be known clearly?"

Common sense demands the answer "Yes." God is good to us, He reveals something of Himself in Creation—obviously He wants to be known. If He wants to be known, He must have found a way to be known accurately.

There must therefore be an objective revelation of God somewhere. It must be written—otherwise it would not be available to everyone in all ages. Where does your neighbor think that an objective written revelation of God might be found?

Common sense tells us that the answer is Christ and the Bible. This is because Christ alone has risen from the dead. Your neighbor needs to see this.

Christ is risen

World religious leaders claim to show the way. Jesus alone claims to *be* the Way. He proved it by His Resurrection. The Resurrection is unique to Christianity. It isn't a healing or resuscitation. Jesus' best friends saw Him alive in a new, physical, and supernatural body.

This is the key proof of Christianity. Happily for us, it is abundantly proved by a mass of evidence to anyone who will use their common sense. The arguments go like this:

The witnesses are reliable

The reporting of any historical event depends upon the

witnesses. The witnesses to the Resurrection are the very best.

1. They couldn't be mistaken. They knew Jesus really well and saw Him regularly—and touched Him—in His resurrected body. It is impossible that they had Him confused with someone else, or that His was just a ghostly body. Some say that He merely fainted on the cross. This is impossible. Crucifixion caused terrible inner injuries. A crucified person could not have appeared three days later as entirely healthy.

2. They wouldn't lie. If they had lied, or been unsure, they would never have witnessed to that resurrection for the rest of their lives. Why not? Because to do so brought persecution, costing all of them pain, and some of them terrible deaths. While alive, they were neither rich nor popular. People simply don't do that for something they know to be a lie.

Witnesses who couldn't be mistaken, and wouldn't lie, must be right. In any case, there is no alternative explanation for the disappearance of Christ's body. Look at the logical alternatives:

(a) It was still in the tomb. Perhaps the disciples had gone to the wrong tomb. But this is impossible. Had the body been available, the authorities would have produced it. Why? Because they wanted to end Christianity, and Jesus' corpse would have done that.

(b) It was taken by the authorities. But had the Jewish or Roman authorities taken the body, they would have produced it, to disprove Christianity.

(c) It was taken by Christians. But this is impossible—why would they die for the truth of His resurrection if they had taken His body?

(d) Grave robbers took the body. This too is impossible. The tomb was found without the body, but with the expensive graveclothes. Why would they leave the most valuable thing? In any case, the tomb was guarded.

The Bible is God's revelation

Christ's Resurrection proves the Bible to be God's objective revelation. How so? Because Christ affirmed the Old Testament (Matt. 5:17-19). He also authorized His apostles, those who were trained by Him and were witnesses of His Resurrection (Acts 1:21-22; 1 Cor. 9:1). The New Testament was seen from the beginning as the work of the apostles or their representatives (Mark and Luke).

Your neighbor may have a host of half-remembered objections to the Bible—"Aren't there contradictions in the Bible?" "Doesn't science disprove the Bible?," etc. Don't be put off by these. They are all easily answered.

"There must be an objective revelation of God," you say. How can God have withheld a clear revelation? "And if it isn't the Bible, what is it?" None of the "sacred books" of the world religions can match the Bible, because none has the miraculous support the Resurrection provides. At the end of the day, they are the opinions of a few men.

Perhaps your neighbor would like to read the Bible with you. Or maybe he would like a Bible in a modern translation, to read himself.

Once he is reading God's Word, he is in direct contact with the truth. Common sense plus Creation has brought him to revelation.

1. Herbert Wolf, "Judges" in *The Expositor's Bible Commentary*, vol. 3 (Zondervan, 1992), 467.
2. Ibid., 466.
3. See Keil on Judges 14:8, in the *Keil & Delitzsch Commentary on the Old Testament*, vol. 2 (reprinted by Eerdmans, 1976), 410.
4. See Dr. Gary North's *Commentary on Leviticus* (Institute for Christian Economics, 1994), 25ff.
5. See the fascinating *Ages in Chaos*, Chapter 3 (Abacus Books, 1952).

5 INITIAL BETRAYAL

Judges 14:15-18

The cheat cheats himself. The Philistines cheated to get the answer to Samson's riddle. But in so doing, they cheated themselves out of an understanding of God's wisdom. Instead, they brought upon themselves His wrath.

This is what happened:

The Philistines didn't really think about the riddle at all. When initially they couldn't understand it, they decided to cheat. They asked Samson's new wife to get the answer out of him. This she agreed to do, and she "wept on him the seven days while their feast lasted" (Jud. 14:17). Meanwhile, the pressure was building on her—by the seventh day, she was being threatened with burning if she didn't get the answer (v. 15).

Samson felt the brunt of her ever-increasing urgency. At last he cracked, and told her the answer. She passed it on, and the Philistines were just in time with the answer to the riddle. They won the bet, but they didn't fool Samson. He realized immediately what had happened. These thirty Philistines were supposed to be his "companions" (v. 11), his friends. They had betrayed that friendship. They were guests at a wedding feast. How had they repaid their host? They had put an obstacle between the newly married couple. Had they no honor? I imagine that they felt their shame when Samson rebuked them.

But they had no choice: they stood to lose money and prestige, and what was their honor next to that?

"If you had not plowed with my heifer, you would not have solved my riddle!" said Samson (v. 18). The meaning is this: Samson's "heifer" is his wife. A heifer is a young animal, normally too young to be used to pull the plow (Deut. 21:3). She would be unused to such harsh treatment. But they had used rough threats on her to force her to betray her husband.

Samson's wife needn't have betrayed her man. Had she brought the matter to him, he could have protected her. He might have called off the wager, or shamed the Philistines into admitting defeat. But she didn't. She didn't understand the true nature of love.

The feast is in full flow. Wherever you look, there is contentment and pleasure. Hard workers are relaxing with friends, surrounded by delicacies and comfort. At the center is the Israelite, with his new bride. They share that special intimacy of love newly consummated.

But as you look, you sense an undercurrent. Things are not as they seem. You look at the guests. It seems that their smiles are too broad, their laughter appears forced. You sense a tension in them; they share an unresolved problem. "What could that problem be?" you wonder. And the way they look at the Israelite—do you see an enmity in those apparently friendly faces?

But his attention is elsewhere. Your face softens as you watch a man with the woman he loves. "The way of a man with a virgin," says the wise man, "is too wonderful for me" (Prov. 30:18-19). You see some of that wonder in their faces.

But even here you sense something wrong. They seem happy enough, but you wonder if all is well. If only you knew how she was in private! She "wept on him, and said, 'You only hate me! You do not love me! You have posed a riddle to the sons of my people, but you have not explained it to me'" (Jud. 14:16).

There is something about a man with a nagging wife; something that you can read as you look at him. Perhaps it's his slight frown; maybe the over-solicitous tone of his voice. And over both of them, he wears an air of disappointment.

We all dream when we fall in love. Sometimes, reality proves even better than the dreams. Sometimes, far worse. It is this that you see in the "happy couple." But perhaps you look away. There are many disappointed marriages; if this is yet another, what of it?

You little imagine that a quarrel is brewing which will soak the land in blood.

What had Samson expected when he married? Presumably, he looked for true love. That was God's pattern from the beginning, and it was his parents' experience too, as we shall see.

God's pattern of true love
At first, God created a man alone (Gen. 2:7). Then He taught the man to long for an ideal companion—the yet uncreated woman (vv. 19-20). His true love would be "a helper comparable to him" (v. 18), a true partner. God chose a special way to create the woman, to emphasize the miracle of true love. He took a rib from the man, thus leaving him incomplete. From this rib He made the woman (vv. 21-22). "Therefore a man shall leave his father and mother and be joined to his wife, and they shall become one flesh" (Gen. 2:24).

The fundamental mystery is this: from two very different and incomplete people a true union comes. This union of lovers is called marriage. It is marvelously fruitful. From it come the children of the next generation; the stable structure of society—and such joy and happiness!

Another way to complete a person is through holy celibacy. Being single gives more time to enjoy wonderful intimacy with Jesus (see 1 Cor. 7).

Our bodies are composed of cells. These cells have amino acids, which are vital for the cells' life. Together, the amino acids flourish. Separate, they die. It is the same with marriage. True marriage is a marvelous miracle, made up of vital parts. If you take it apart, it dies. None of the parts keeps its wonderment alone.

These are the parts: love, marriage, and sexual relations. "Love" is the passionate giving of oneself. "I am my beloved's," it says, "and my beloved is mine" (Song of Songs 6:3). This is not a loan; it is not a partial or temporary present. It is far beyond such petty matters. True love gives completely, exclusively, and forever.

Marriage is the public and outward expression of this life-long love. It is a binding covenant made before God. "So then, they are no longer two but one flesh. Therefore what God has joined together, let not man separate" (Matt. 19:6). Anyone breaking a marriage covenant is sinning against God (Ps. 51:4)—and God will deal with them: "Marriage is honorable among all, and the bed undefiled; but fornicators and adulterers God will judge" (Heb. 13:4).

The third part is sexual relations. Love joins the hearts; marriage joins the outward lives—sexual relations joins the bodies. God designed sexual relations for the enjoyment of married lovers.

These three parts are one, just as you have a heart, a life, and a body. Separate these and you die.

Strangers to love

The Philistines seem hardly to have had a glimpse of true love. When Abraham met them centuries before, they knew nothing of it. Abraham's wife Sarah was "a woman of beautiful countenance" (Gen. 12:11), and he feared for his wife—and his life. He expected them to kill him and take her, so he pretended that she was his sister.

Sure enough, the Philistine king "sent and took Sarah" (Gen. 20:2). What an ugly expression! True love gives; it seeks; it asks—it doesn't come and take. God gave the king a shock. Perhaps the Philistines learned a lesson, because we find them, in the next generation, aware of the holiness of marriage (Gen. 26:6-11).

In Samson's time, the Philistines appeared to have lost all knowledge of true love. Did Samson's wife give herself to him? Hardly: she refused to be one with him, and took her kinsfolk's side. She manipulated his emotions—"she had wept on him the seven days while their feast lasted" (Jud. 14:17). Then she betrayed him. She could not say, "I am my beloved's."

Samson's "anger was aroused, and he went back up to his father's house" (Jud. 14:19). This is hardly surprising. But however disappointed he was, Samson had no intention of breaking the marriage covenant. So he returned to her later, with a present. To his amazement, her father had given her as "wife" to the best man! (v. 20) Since she was still married to Samson in his (and God's) eyes, this was nothing less than legalized adultery. But her father felt no shame. He simply offered Samson his next daughter as wife! (15:2) We shall see what Samson thought of that.

Through this sorry tale, one thing remains constant. The Philistines knew nothing of true love.

We are never told Samson's feelings. Perhaps you can guess at them. He marries the woman he loves. She manipulates him, deceives him, and betrays him—and all on the honeymoon. When he sees her next, she is living with another man.

"Samson should have known what to expect," you say. "After all, she was a Philistine." True. But young men make mistakes, and sometimes come out of them unscathed. Samson came out devastated. Perhaps a little pity is in order.

If you have any compassion to spare, there are many who seek it. Today there are "Samsons" without number: men and women whose spouses have left them. I believe that God's people should reach out to them with love and understanding.

I believe too that the notion of true love is disappearing from our culture. We have the secret, and we need to keep it in the public eye. Most of all, we need to make sure that the Philistine way doesn't infiltrate our lives.

The demise of true love

In the '60s, the cry was for "free love." It turned out to be "Philistine love," or even "freedom from love." It meant that the vital parts of true love were separated.

The "sexual revolution" meant that sex would be separated from love and marriage. Sex was simply a physical act that was enjoyable. In reality, however, sex joins a man and woman in body as "one flesh." This is so, even with a prostitute: "Do you not know that he who is joined to a harlot is one body with her? For 'the two,' He says, 'shall become one flesh'" (1 Cor. 6:16).

There is great pressure on people to be sexually immoral. Subconsciously, our humanistic society wants everyone initiated into Philistine ways. It can be hard for young people to resist, but they must. "Flee sexual immorality," says the apostle. "Every sin that a man does is outside the body, but he who commits sexual immorality sins against his own body" (1 Cor. 6:18). They become less able to truly love, because their bodies are already joined to other people. It all seemed so easy at the time! Perhaps they thought: "I can always repent later." It is not quite as easy as that. I have prayed with some young people on the eve of their marriages, where the memory of their immorality had become bitter now that they saw it reaching forward and marring their future happiness. Thank God for the tears of true repentance! Thank God for restoration! But never take these things lightly.

The "sexual revolution" treated marriage in Philistine fashion. Although the love song said "I will always love you," adultery denied the "always." Ironically, the excuse for adultery was love: "I don't love you anymore—I love *her* now." In reality, true love was disappearing. The old song got it right: "When I fall in love, it will be forever." Another line goes: "When I give my heart, it will be completely."

Errors breed their opposites. If people thought of love and sex without marriage, then soon there was marriage without love and sex. Today's style seems: first to like each other, then to share sexual intimacy, then to live together. One gets the impression that when couples marry, the romance soon ends. Statistics suggest that sexual intimacy within marriage is far less than one might expect—and sometimes ceases altogether.

Sin is not just wrong—it is miserable! The legacy of Philistine love is a sad one. After all the "free love" and sexual immorality, what do we have? The glad dawn of freedom promised in the '60s never came. We are left with broken families, broken society, broken hearts, broken promises, broken health, and broken dreams.

Competition
True love is under attack today in a way unknown to the

Philistines. Instead of true lovers completing each other, couples are competing with each other.

As we saw, woman was created from man's rib. This shows us that men and women are different, each supplying what is missing in the other. They are like parts of a Chinese puzzle. A Chinese puzzle has funny-shaped bits that form a whole when they are fitted together. The hard part is finding how to fit them together.

God has told us how true lovers fit together: "Wives, submit to your own husbands, as to the Lord. . . . Husbands, love your wives, just as Christ also loved the church and gave Himself for her" (Eph. 5:22-25).

This is the true solution to the puzzle. It is essential if true love is to flourish.

Why is that? It is because true lovers give themselves fully to each other. This complete giving means that each wants to make the other happy. If there must be a sacrifice, each wants to make it for the other. This could cause the same deadlock as two selfish people trying to get their own way. But if their joint life is to flow freely, then someone must take the lead. God has told us that the man is in charge—and is to use his authority in a sacrificial manner, "just as Christ also loved the church and gave Himself for her."

Humanism, quick to dispense with God's authority, demoted all whom He had appointed. The husband was no longer the "head of the wife." So, who would now be in charge?

This is where the competing came in. Nature demands that someone be at the wheel, and selfishness demands it be me. Why me? Because if it were you, I would be at your mercy. I just want to be sure I'm safe—that I won't be trodden down.

How do people compete? The man usually has greater physical strength, but the woman (like Samson's wife) can manipulate him with tears. "You do not love me!" she says (Jud. 14:16). They both know that Samson loves her; that's why such a tactic works. He can't bear to see her unhappy; he is desperate that she should know how much he loves her.

What is going through her mind? If you had asked her if she loved her man, she would probably have said "Yes." But it isn't true love—she isn't her beloved's. How can she give herself to him while she is manipulating him? She is clearly determined to have the control in the marriage; she is competing, not completing.

Wifely submission and the sacrificial headship of the husband—these are rejected with disdain today. Many see them as a constraint from which women ought to be liberated. They are viewed as a heartless male domination, imposed by superstitious religion. In reality, God's pattern is vital if true lovers are to *complete* each other—if true love is to flourish.

Some non-Christians know true love, and some Christians appear not to. Nevertheless, I believe it is up to us to live it and show it to a loveless world.

The church's witness to true love

True love is intensely private. But its fruit is visible to all. Husband and wife are visibly united in a loving union. We can see this oneness in Samson's parents. Samson's mother had been barren when unexpectedly, an angel appeared to her. She is to have a son, she is told, and he must be a life-long Nazirite. Now we see her reaction to this astonishing appearance: "The woman came and told her husband" (Jud. 13:6). Unlike Samson's wife, this true lover immediately shares with her husband, Manoah. As head of his wife, Manoah wants to hear the message himself, and prays accordingly. Sure enough, the angel returns. He appears to Manoah's wife. She knows her husband wants to speak to the angel, so what does she do?

"The woman ran in haste and told her husband" (v. 10). She "ran in haste," so eager to tell her husband, whom she loved. The angel disappears with a display of glory. Manoah is terrified, and says to his wife, "We shall surely die, because we have seen God!" (v. 22) Fear has confused his thinking; but all is well. His wife puts him straight with her wisdom and clarity (v. 23). Her submission is not one of slavery. Had it been so, all she would have said is "Yes, dear." Her submission is that of *true love*. When he panics, his wife comforts him and supplies the calm wisdom that he lacks.

It seems to me that many young people today are doomed never to know true love. They are under pressure to be sexually active; they expect to live with a partner before marriage; they are warned not to give their hearts, lest they be "controlled." The three vital parts of true love are hopelessly split. What hope have they?

God's church is the guardian of true love. Not only do we proclaim the love of God, but we display His pattern for true love on earth.

Look for a true lover

We must learn from Samson's unhappiness. We must make sure that *our* marriages aren't "Philistine." Young people need all the help and advice they can get. In my experience, evangelical Christians have been a vital source of pointers to a happy marriage:

1. Choose a fellow believer

We are to marry "only in the Lord" (1 Cor. 7:39). "Do not be unequally yoked together with unbelievers," we are told (2 Cor. 6:14), for "what part has a believer with an unbeliever?" (v. 15)

Christians are warned that marriage with a nonbeliever will bring a conflict of priorities. The things at the top of your list—God's will, the church, evangelism—probably wouldn't appear on your spouse's at all. This is bound to lead to trouble.

2. Stay pure before marriage

Christians are commanded in Scripture to remain virgins until marriage. An engaged couple who plead that "we are getting married and we really love each other!" are reminded that sex outside marriage is fornication—seriously offensive to God (1 Cor. 6:9). Clearly, it is easier to resist a temptation before it is at its strongest. The evangelical counsel has therefore been to "flee also youthful lusts" (2 Tim. 2:22) by avoiding what is likely to increase temptation.

3. Marry a friend

Just because someone is sexually attractive and a fellow believer, doesn't mean that life together would be bliss. Do you enjoy being together? Do you laugh at the same jokes, share the same interests? Is this someone you would choose as a companion for life?

Are we missing something?

Of course, we would always ask a young couple contemplating marriage whether they loved one another. And they would say "Yes." But that doesn't mean that they know what true love is.

It is true that we can be overcautious. A young couple got married and went away to a beautiful resort for their honeymoon. Once there, they found that they had spent so long repenting of their sexual feelings that they couldn't change—even though they were now married. Things were sorted out for them, but they aren't for everyone.

I once heard a wonderful missionary speaking to a group of Christian young people. He warned them against sexual relations before marriage. To avoid it, he told them that they mustn't even hold hands before marriage! The way he said it, it sounded like God's command rather than the missionary's opinion. But where does the Bible say this?

"Anything that helps young people stay pure must be good," someone says. But we must remember how the Devil works. There are always errors on both sides of the truth. The true way is a narrow road—and there is a ditch on either side.

Let me give you another example. There was a woman who had become engaged to a young man in the church youth group. They were both Christians, and good friends. They made sure to avoid sexual relations before marriage. In due course, they got married. On the wedding night, the woman found to her horror that she couldn't give herself to her husband. She just didn't want him to touch her. It was the same the following night. In fact, after five years the marriage was annulled—it had never been consummated. It wasn't that she didn't like him; she just couldn't give herself to him. She wasn't truly in love with him.

I know a minister who followed the three evangelical guidelines when he fell in love. Once married, he found something missing. His wife wasn't completely his, on any level. For many years he longed that she would truly love him. Like Samson, he found that his love for her allowed her to manipulate him. Eventually, she left him for another man. When she left, she told him that she had never loved him.

We should emphasize true love
I believe that we should teach young people what the Bible says about the holy wonders of true love. On the one hand, we must tell them *not* to give themselves to each other before marriage.

But to keep the balance, we should show them how true love gives itself so fully and joyfully in marriage. A marriage where there is no true giving of each to the other is displeasing to God (1 Cor. 7:3-5). Sexual immorality is a danger, but it is not the only danger. In any case, true love is one good reason for keeping oneself pure. If you were just about to enjoy the most wonderful meal of your life, would you ruin it by eating a bowlful of pretzels?

In fact, imbalance is always self-defeating. If we speak mainly of the dangers of sexual desire, then the world will speak about the ecstasies of love. Young people will think that Christians have purity and sinners have ecstasy! What a lie that is! The truth is that the pure are happy (Matt. 5:8). True love belongs to God, not the Devil.

Sinners can keep their perversion, their loveless sex, and whatever else. We are satisfied with true love.

As far as we know, Samson never in his whole life found a woman who truly loved him. This is very sad, but it isn't the saddest thing of all. Many people never in their whole lives find the God who is Love. This is far sadder. So matters of true love must be kept in proportion. Samson will spend eternity enjoying the love of God. Against that, his earthly sufferings are not worth noticing.

TRUE JUSTICE

6

Judges 14:19–15:8

Samson "judged Israel twenty years in the days of the Philistines" (Jud. 15:20). If we are to understand what Samson did, we need to know what a judge was.

We call Old Testament Israel a "theocracy." That means that God ruled the country. God ruled through His law, the revelation of right and wrong which we have in Exodus to Deuteronomy. God's action didn't mean man's inaction. There were to be men who applied God's law in the innumerable situations of everyday life.

The "teaching priest" (2 Chron. 15:3) was to "devote himself to the law of the Lord" (2 Chron. 31:4). Thus it was that "the lips of a priest should keep knowledge, and people should seek the law from his mouth; for he is the messenger of the Lord of hosts" (Mal. 2:7).

But there would be cases where people were in dispute. No doubt, where money or rights were at stake, wise men were needed to interpret God's law in the specific case. These men were called judges. They were to be chosen by the people (Deut. 1:13) for their wisdom and integrity (Ex 18:20-22). Their job was to "judge the people at all times" (v. 22) on the basis of God's Law (v. 20).

When Israel was unfaithful to God, He permitted pagan nations to enslave them. Obviously a different law—an idolatrous one—replaced the holy Law of God. When God raised up leaders to rescue His people, they were called judges.

Why "judges," and not "rescuers" or "revolutionaries"? The reason is that God wanted people to understand what He was doing. He wasn't just ridding the land of invaders; He was reintroducing His law. These judges defeated the enemy. They also acted as the highest law court in the land.

We are told, for instance, that Samuel "judged Israel all the days of his life" (1 Sam. 7:15). Specifically, "He went from year to year on a circuit to Bethel, Gilgal, and Mizpah, and judged Israel in all those places" (v. 16). He fought one battle to free Israel. But he spent all the rest of his time doing the work of a judge. Samson was the same. The time between fights with the Philistines was spent judging Israel "twenty years" (Jud. 15:20).

The system of judges worked like this: there was a judge to hear cases for everyone. The lesser judges worked among small communities—"rulers of tens" (Ex. 18:21), the greater judges served much larger groups, up to "thousands." When a case was too hard, it would be sent up to a higher judge—the highest judge originally being Moses (Ex. 18:22).

That meant that Samson had only to hear the hardest cases—lesser judges coped with easier matters. As chief judge, Samson would have had to make sure that God's law was known, just as Moses did (Ex. 18:20).

We are to imagine Samson, therefore, as a wise man. He sifted through the Word of God, and found righteous solutions. Yes, Samson was a man of action. But that wasn't his daily duty—extraordinary circumstances called forth extraordinary actions. Ordinarily, he judged the people according to the Word of God.

Samson began to "judge Israel" after the victory of Ramath Lehi, as we shall see. But he bursts on the scene as a judge in the events of this chapter. That is why the Holy Spirit strengthened him to kill Philistines (Jud. 14:19; 15:14); it is as a judge that he killed them.

God the Judge of all

Something else was happening among the Philistines at around the same time.[1]

As we saw earlier, the ark of the covenant was captured by the Philistines after Israel's defeat in battle. The Philistines returned the ark to Israel, but that was seven months later.

What happened over those seven months? We find the story in 1 Samuel 5–6.

Pagans thought in terms of small-scale gods, each trying to further the cause of their devotees. A battle between the Philistines and Israel was seen as a battle between respective gods—Dagon versus Jehovah. Each side was eager for its own god to win.

In reality, Jehovah is the God of the whole earth. He permitted Israel to lose, to teach them not to be idolatrous (Jud. 13:1). God was using the Philistines for His own purposes, but they didn't realize it. Like Assyria later on, they thought: "By the strength of my hand I have done it" (Isa. 10:13). To the Assyrians, God said:

> Shall the ax boast itself against him who chops with it?
> Or shall the saw exalt itself against him who
> saws with it?
> As if a rod could wield itself against those who
> lift it up,
> Or as if a staff could lift up, as if it were not
> wood! (v. 15)

The same applied to the Philistines. They became unbearably arrogant, and God had to clarify their viewpoint.

Dagon bites the dust

The Philistines put Jehovah's ark in the house of Dagon in Ashdod, and "set it by Dagon" (1 Sam. 5:2). Presumably, it was a "thank-you" gift to Dagon for defeating Jehovah. Next morning, the statue of Dagon was on its face before the ark of the God of the whole earth.

This must have been very disconcerting for the Philistines, but they replaced the statue and hoped for the best. The next morning, they found the statue in the same position, but with head and hands broken off.

At this point, the Philistines in Ashdod felt it was time for the ark to go. In any case, they were already feeling the hand of God. "The hand of the Lord was heavy on the people of Ashdod, and he ravaged them and struck them with tumors, both Ashdod and its territory" (1 Sam. 5:6). We don't know what sort of tumors these were (they proved fatal for some, v. 12)—but the Philistines certainly got the message.

It was thought best to move the ark to another Philistine city, Gath. But the same thing happened there. When the ark arrived at Ekron, the next Philistine city, no one was glad to see it. "They have brought the ark of the God of Israel to us, to kill us and our people!" the Ekronites cried (1 Sam. 5:10).

The trophy of victory had now become a symbol of impotence. The Israelites might not be much in battle, but their God was terrifying. The Philistines were in crisis. They determined to return the ark, with a "trespass offering" (1 Sam. 6:3; see also Leviticus 5). They were well aware of what God had done in the Exodus (1 Sam. 6:6), and didn't want to antagonize Him any further.

The ark was returned to Beth Shemesh in Israel. But the story doesn't end there.

Judgment at the house of God

The Israelites of Beth Shemesh greeted the ark with suitable reverence. But the reverence didn't last for long. They couldn't resist having a look in the ark—something they knew was forbidden. God killed 50,070 men as punishment—more than had died in the battle against the Philistines (compare 1 Sam. 4:10 and 6:19).

Fifty thousand people! That is probably many more than had died from the tumors in the Philistine cities. This should not surprise us. God says: "The time has come for judgment to begin at the house of God" (1 Peter 4:17). He expects more from His own people. "For everyone to whom much is given, from him much will be required; and to whom much has been committed, of him they will ask the more" (Luke 12:48).

After that, the ark was moved to Kiriath Jearim, where Samson was based (1 Sam. 7:1; see also Jud. 13:25 and 18:12).

The Judge's judge

For the Philistines, this was a time of judgment. They had been permitted to overcome God's people, because they were unholy. But God's ark wasn't unholy, and they had been judged for taking it. They were faced with "God the Judge of all" (Heb. 12:23), and they weren't enjoying it.

But the Judge had a judge too—Samson. Samson was different from his unholy countryfolk. He stood for God's Law. He brought judgment by the power of the Spirit. There were three judgments:

1. Judgment on idolaters

"Then the Spirit of the Lord came upon him mightily, and he went down to Ashkelon and killed thirty of their men, took their apparel, and gave the changes of clothing to those who had explained the riddle" (Jud. 14:19).

Why did he go to Ashkelon? It was one of the five major

Philistine cities, about twenty miles away. It was a long way to carry thirty suits of clothes. Here are my conclusions:

(a) He wasn't motivated by personal vengeance—otherwise he would have killed some local Philistines, since it was they who had wronged him.

(b) He wasn't trying to keep the killing quiet—otherwise he would have stayed away from a major center.

(c) He didn't kill to get the clothes. Obviously it is far easier to get clothes without killing for them—by stealing them, for instance. Samson was never armed, so there would be a danger of ruining the clothes in the process of killing their wearers.

(d) He did no wrong. This is obvious, because the Spirit doesn't empower wicked actions.

I agree with the great Bible commentator Matthew Henry that Samson went to Ashkelon because "probably he knew there was some great festival observed at this time, to which many flocked."[2] Pagans going to an idolatrous festival would be wearing special clothes. But it wouldn't have been righteous to kill people for their clothes.

God had established a law for the Promised Land that no one could encourage people to worship false gods. Ashkelon was in the Promised Land. The penalty was death (see Deut. 13:12-15). This is clearly a merciful law; it protects people from being seduced into false religion, and thence into hell. The bodily death of a few is far better than eternal torment for many. This explains why our loving God instituted the death penalty (Matt. 15:4; Rom. 1:32; 13:4).

I imagine something like this: Samson realizes that he must find thirty suits of clothing. He cannot afford them, and he will not steal them. He realizes that there are at least thirty people deserving of capital punishment twenty miles away. He knows that he has been called as a judge to deliver Israel from the

Philistines. He has the right—even the obligation—to execute these men, but does he have the courage?

Can he go into a Philistine city full of people, and execute thirty men? Not without the power of God—but this is soon provided, when "the Spirit of the Lord came upon him mightily." The property of these idolaters is forfeit (Deut. 13:16), so he takes the clothing he needs, and brings it back to Timnah.

2. Judgment on thieves

When things had calmed down and Samson returned for his wife, he found her given to the best man in an adulterous "marriage." His father-in-law had betrayed him—and stolen from him. In those days, a bridegroom would give a brideprice to the bride's father, as part of the wedding arrangements. For Jacob, this had been seven years of free labor (Gen. 29:18).

No doubt this money became part of the general wealth of the family, but if the husband ever left the wife, he lost it forever. But Samson had not broken his marriage. He had merely stormed out in anger, and then returned. Samson's father-in-law had evidently taken Samson's wife, and not returned the brideprice. But he was not solely at fault; the whole community had presumably approved the theft.

Justice demanded the return of the money. If it were a sum equivalent to seven years' wages, it would be a substantial amount. And remember that a thief must restore double what he stole (Ex. 22:4). Samson didn't want the money, as we shall see, but a judge has to see justice done. But how could he get the community to restore what they owed?

In the event, Samson devised a remarkable scheme. He caught 300 foxes—not an easy task in itself—and tied their tails together in pairs. I sometimes see a fox where I live. They are very timid of humans; even though you stand completely still, they are poised for flight. The slightest movement, and they are gone. They can be damaging pests: "Catch us the foxes, the little foxes that spoil the vines" (Song 2:15).

When Samson releases the foxes, they flee as quickly as they can. Tied together, I imagine their course is highly erratic. Samson has attached a burning torch to their tails, so they spread fire wherever they run. . . .

For a while the fire goes unnoticed. Then—a shout! "The grain's on fire!" someone cries. The flames are now clearly visible, leaping up in the grain fields, among the vines and the olives.

Is someone starting the fires? Impossible—no one could move so fast: new fires are springing up everywhere you look. Anyway, a firestarter would be clearly visible, unless he were crawling on his face. Is this the wrath of some god? Why are the fields catching fire on every side?

Then they see it: two foxes tied together, with a burning torch dragging behind them. "Catch them! Stop them!" they yell. They are racing towards the field, each one busy protecting their own property. But it's no good. The foxes are like creatures with one body but two brains. They are terrified: the presence of humans would have scared them, but now there is the fire, the smoke, and the shouting. Each fox panics, and pulls in its own direction. They are so fast!

Soon everyone is coughing in the smoke. The double-foxes seem to be everywhere. All the fields are ablaze; the harvest is lost. Wherever we look, we see shouting men; running men; angry men; blackened men.

On the hill above a lone figure stands watching. The strange arrangement of his hair strikes them, "The riddling Israelite," they murmur. He had been quiet when he was told he wouldn't be getting his brideprice back. "Justice demands you pay," he had stated in a quiet voice.

Now he stands observing the bedlam. They look again at the foxes. "Just the kind of trick that crafty riddler would dream up," they think.

Someone will have to pay for the lost harvest. Their gaze returns to the lone figure. A kind of menace hangs over him.

Someone else will have to pay.

The Philistine community decided that Samson had been wronged, and they didn't seem to blame him for the episode of the foxes. But someone had to pay; so they burned his wife and father-in-law to death.

If they thought their cruel vengeance would placate him, they were very wrong. He had not sought personal revenge. Justice was his aim: "This time I shall be blameless regarding the Philistines if I harm them!" he had said (Jud. 15:3). "Blameless" here is a legal word.

But the Philistines' cruelty was anything but legal.

3. Judgment on murderers

Killing Samson's wife and father-in-law was murder. "But surely," someone will say, "isn't death the penalty for adultery?"—and clearly this "marriage" was adulterous.

We know that God had said: "The man who commits adultery with another man's wife, he who commits adultery with his neighbor's wife, the adulterer and the adulteress, shall surely be put to death" (Lev. 20:10).

But the Philistines acted like the Pharisees. The Pharisees brought a woman to Jesus and said: "Teacher, this woman was caught in adultery, in the very act" (John 8:4). Was she alone in the act of adultery? No? Then where was the man? The Bible makes clear that both "the adulterer and the adulteress" are equally guilty, equally liable to death. There is no justice in executing just one of them.

The Philistines weren't interested in justice—otherwise they would have punished both the guilty. They were interested in revenge, so they killed the ones they thought had provoked Samson. And that is murder.

The distinction is between justice and personal revenge. When Samson said: "Since you would do a thing like this, I will surely take revenge on you, and after that I will cease" (Jud. 15:7), he was speaking of justice. The Hebrew word for revenge, *naqam*, is a legal word. It speaks of lawful punishment, not personal revenge.

Once Samson had exacted the legitimate penalty, he "would cease." By contrast, we know that vendettas go on for generations.

The penalty for murder is death. Samson "attacked them hip and thigh with a great slaughter" (Jud. 15:8). We have no clues to the details of this just punishment, except that it was "hip and thigh"—or, literally, "hip *on* thigh." "Hip" is often translated "leg," as in Psalm 147:10: "He does not delight in the strength of the horse; he takes no pleasure in the legs of a man." The leg is where man's most powerful muscle is found.

"Thigh" is often translated "side." We should imagine Samson, unarmed, kicking the Philistines in their sides. Richard Rogers (A.D. 1615) thought that Samson "so lamed and pained with kicking them with his feet, that he did beat life out of them."[3]

This form of combat is associated with martial arts today, and is the subject of many popular films. Today's movie fans would be surprised to learn that the greatest martial arts hero of them all was Samson. But the filmmakers have no idea of the real secret of strength.

There is no reason to doubt that Samson's opponents were armed—but it was to no avail.

Loving justice and lawless "love"

In this chapter we have seen God bringing legal punishment on the Philistines, and His judge, Samson, doing the same. These punishments were made on the basis of God's holy Law.

We need to understand true justice. We must live in terms of it; we must vote for a government that exercises it. But living as we do in a humanistic age, we live with a confusing notion—humanistic "love." In Bible terms, it is a lawless love.

Old paganism knew nothing of selfless love. When the pagans saw that the church was out to conquer the world through love, they thought it ridiculous. Christians cared for the poor and needy, Christian or pagan. How could they win any battles that way? But God used this selfless love to pierce the heart of many a pagan sinner. Faced with something truly beautiful, they repented, and the Roman Empire bowed the knee before the Carpenter.

Modern paganism has learned its lesson. It speaks much of "love" and "caring." It must—otherwise it is doomed.

The difference between this "love" and the Christlike love of the church is this: humanistic love is lawless. "Love is the fulfillment of the Law," says the Holy Spirit (Rom. 13:10). In other words, the genuine expression of love will coincide with what God has commanded in the Bible.

This is what I mean: if I love God, I will try to please Him. What pleases God? Is it up to me to decide that? Of course not—God Himself has revealed what He wants in the Bible. "For this is the love of God, that we keep His commandments" (1 John 5:3).

Genuine love for God means doing what He says He likes—not what I say He likes. Everyone and everything has been made by God. So God defines how we should love our neighbor. "By this we know that we love the children of God, when we love God and keep His commandments" (1 John 5:2). God shows us in the Word how we can love each other.

Suppose you ask me to get you some heroin. Is it "love" if I do so? Of course not—the heroin will harm you, even kill you. Just because you want something, it doesn't mean that it is good for you. I truly love you "when I love God and keep His commandments"—that is, when I do things for you that fit with the Bible.

Later on, we shall see Delilah begging Samson to do something. "How can you say, 'I love you? . . .'" she said as she manipulated him (Jud. 16:15). Samson eventually did what she wanted, but it wasn't love because it wasn't God's will.

How does all this apply to us?

A lawless society

We can see many examples of lawless love in our own society. At times, lawless love protects the guilty and exposes the innocent.

One example is "free love." Our society allows—even admires—adulterous and immoral relationships. "What harm is done," they ask, "when consenting adults do whatever they enjoy? Live and let live!" It seems to be "love" to remove the prohibitions. By contrast, the Christian appears to lack tolerance, and hence is deemed unloving.

In practice, adultery breaks marriages. The result? The sorrows of so many single-parent families. Let's add up the cost of this lawless love. There is the anguish of the innocent party, whom the adulterer betrays. This innocent party may become depressed and need treatment, at the tax payers' expense. Then there is the single-parent family. Many are without the income of the adulterous spouse, and must be supported by welfare.

Why am I talking about financial burdens, when there is so much suffering? It is because money—unlike suffering—is easily calculated. People as a whole suffer from "free love"—and the cost to the taxpayer expresses it in a visible way. Ordinary people may be innocent of the adultery, but they still foot the bill. But this burden is slight next to that of the children. They have lost a parent—perhaps it is the innocent one—who no longer lives with them. These children are paying for the freedom of adulterers to break their vows.

Is this love? No—it is lawlessness.

By contrast, God's Law in the Bible seems harsh—but it is only harsh toward the guilty. Even that harshness contains mercy, since it directs the guilty toward repentance and life. With God, there is no footing of the bill on the part of the innocent. That is the theme of Ezekiel 18, which ends with this appeal: "I have no pleasure in the death of one who dies . . . therefore turn and live!" (v. 32)

Christians in a democratic society

It has been observed that lobbyists can have a huge impact within the democratic system, and our society certainly needs a huge impact! We are the people to make it. Too often, we embrace the political views of our pagan society. Are you on the left or the right? Neither, I hope. Neither left nor right rises above lawless love. When it comes to politics, I trust you are with Jesus.

What is my point? We all agree that when it comes to our lives, God tells us how to run them. I am saying that the same applies to politics. Only God knows how best to run the country.

Political systems are derived from one's underlying assumptions. This is true of both left and right. Whatever their roots in our country's Christian heritage, or in caring policies—neither acknowledges God's absolute authority. If we identify ourselves fully with either, we are identifying with their disobedience to God.[4] I am not saying that everything in either system is wrong;

nor that left or right is without sincere Christian components. It is simply that we should base our politics on the Bible. This is far from easy, so how do we do it?

Which are the biblical policies?
The great masters of the word have worked hard to expound the scriptural pattern for our lives. By contrast, very little work has been done on analyzing the biblical message for politicians. Currently, as I write, all this is changing. It is, however, far from easy to apply the Word to today's society.

Why is this? The fundamental Scriptures (Exodus to Deuteronomy) are set in an agricultural society, with land belonging inalienably to Israel's families. Our society is different in almost every way. We know that God has given us all we need in His Word—but we have much work to do in applying it with confidence.

The best thing we can do is to hold out for the best. However we vote at the present time, let it be known that we are waiting for a political party which is true to God. We think it will be best for the country—the whole country, Christians and pagans alike. There are a lot of us Christians around, and there are more all the time. Sooner or later, someone is going to offer what we want—and they'll get themselves elected.

Meanwhile, let's agree on the things that are clear. For instance, it is clearly wrong to kill unborn babies (Ex. 21:22-24). We can agree on that, and campaign together. Whatever you do, do not allow yourself to be muzzled. Don't let the humanists restrict you to humanistic left or humanistic right. This is a democratic society, so use your vote.

Does God have a vote?
Even if Christians have been persuaded to support the policies

of pagans, left or right, God hasn't. He remains Judge. We need to see how He exercises His sovereign authority. We are familiar with the way God judged His own people in Bible times. Israel regularly felt the firmness of God's hand. There were national judgments: defeat, enslavement, exile.

God threatens a wide range of judgments if His people betray Him. We find these listed in Leviticus 26 and Deuteronomy 28. These include sickness, mental illness, poverty, exposure to violence, and much else. That these judgments were intended seriously is clear from the biblical histories.

Some have declared (or hoped) that these judgments applied only to Israel, but it is not so.

> For the land is defiled; therefore I visit the punishment of its iniquity upon it, and the land vomits out its inhabitants. You shall therefore keep My statutes and My judgments, and shall not commit any of these abominations, either any of your own nation or any stranger who dwells among you (for all these abominations the men of the land have done, who were before you, and thus the land is defiled), lest the land vomit you out also when you defile it, as it vomited out the nations that were before you (Lev. 18:25-28).

Here we are told that the original inhabitants of the land—the Canaanites—were punished for breaking the same laws that God commanded Israel. If Israel broke these laws, she too would be punished. Many nations are judged and punished in the Bible (see, for instance, Jer. 46–51). Is our nation being punished today? What do you think? Run your eye down this list:

Suicide: more common than ever before, particularly among the young.
Drug abuse: this self-afflicted epidemic affects the whole Western world.
Recession: financial recessions bring poverty to poorer groups in the affluent West.
Crime: violent crime making many feel unsafe.
Broken families: marital infidelity breaking down the stability of society, once family-based.
Sickness: in spite of medical science, and the longer life span, the nation seems less healthy nowadays.
Debt: from governments to ordinary people, everyone seems to owe something.
Dishonesty: there was a time when you could trust the ordinary person.

The list could be extended. As a minister, I have listened to many who were brought up in the early decades of this century. Their memories are living history books. They all speak of lowered standards. Technology has brought so many blessings, but things seem worse in other areas.

Christians are busy helping the afflicted in all these areas, as we should be. But if the increasing godlessness of our nations is the reason for this suffering, shouldn't we be speaking out about it?

Yes, God does have a vote. He voted against the Philistines removing His ark from Israel. He sent Samson, His judge, to make public His hatred of idolatry, theft, and murder.

An eye or not an eye?
I am often asked to reconcile Jesus' words with those of Moses. Jesus said:

You have heard that it was said, "An eye for an eye and a tooth for a tooth." But I tell you not to resist an evil person. But whoever slaps you on your right cheek, turn the other to him also (Matt. 5:38-39).

Moses had written:

But if any harm follows, then you shall give life for life, eye for eye, tooth for tooth, hand for hand, foot for foot, burn for burn, wound for wound, stripe for stripe (Ex. 21:23-25).

These two Scriptures are easily harmonized, but it is significant that Christians have problems with them. Whenever I am asked, it reminds me that we are being brainwashed into keeping the Bible out of politics. Humanists don't mind us applying the Bible to our personal lives, but would rather we left them to run our country.

The fact is that Moses is speaking about a political issue, while Jesus is speaking about our personal lives. God used Moses to shape a nation. When Jesus said "But I tell you . . ." He was talking to a remnant of believers, not the legislators of a nation. That is why Jesus appears to contradict what He, as God the Son, had already said through Moses. God's directives for legislators and judges are different from what He commands private citizens.

Suppose a Christian were also a judge. If that Christian were insulted on his way to work, he would "turn the other cheek." He would be acting as a private citizen; he would forgive the personal insult. But once he is at work, everything changes. As a judge, he is not acting as a private citizen. If a criminal comes before him, he cannot pardon him. What would happen in our land if murderers were pardoned and allowed to go free?

In Moses' day, God was setting up an entirely new society. He gave Moses the blueprints for it. But Jesus taught when Israel was part of the Roman Empire. He didn't speak about the best pattern for society; He showed us how to live under unrighteous laws.

So there is no contradiction between Moses and Jesus. How could there be? "If you believed Moses," Jesus said, "you would believe Me; for he wrote about Me" (John 5:46).

Living by the high rule of true justice

Few of us are called, as Samson was, to high political office. But we are all involved, because we may all vote. Let us take our responsibility seriously. So far as our private lives are concerned, let us remember to seek God's Word rather than follow our own idea of what constitutes love.

Let me give some examples. Some time ago, a Christian woman came to me with a problem. She had been shopping with a friend and the friend wanted to buy something, but didn't have the money. The Christian was asked to buy it, using her credit card. "I'll get the money to you before you get the credit card bill," was the promise.

But time had passed, and the Christian still hadn't received the money—and she couldn't pay her bill.

What had gone wrong? She felt she was being loving when she allowed her friend to use the credit card, but now it had all backfired. But is it loving to become the guarantor of a friend's debts? The Holy Spirit says not (see Prov. 6:1-5). My Christian friend never got her money back—but perhaps she learned that God, not human sentiment, defines what love is.

As I shared this in our Bible college, a student responded

with amazement. He had become a business partner with another man, and was now liable for any debts that his partner might incur. His partner had proved unreliable, and the student had felt an inner prompting to dissolve the partnership.

He had wondered about this inner prompting, but never realized that God had spoken of these matters in the Bible. He was gripped with a sudden excitement. He had discovered that "Your commandment is exceedingly broad" (Ps. 119:96)—and covers a wider area than he had thought.

These are simply two of a great many examples. We, the dear children of God, need to know His will in the infallible Scriptures. If we have a working knowledge of the Word of God, we will know where to look for answers.

If we seek God's way in all the areas of our lives, then we shall be blessed. Look again at Leviticus 26 and Deuteronomy 28, and see what blessings God promises to the obedient.

"Blessed are those who hunger and thirst for righteousness, for they shall be filled" (Matt. 5:6).

---

1. See the appendix. The traditional chronology puts these events in the same year.
2. See Matthew Henry's *Commentary on Judges* 14:19.
3. See Rogers' Commentary on Judges (Banner of Truth, facsimile 1983), 704. I have modernized the spelling.
4. See this expounded in detail in Dr. Gary North's *Political Polytheism* (Institute for Christian Economics, 1989).

7 VALOR'S FINEST VICTORY

Judges 15:9-15

When I was a child, I used to admire the stories of heroic courage. I must only have been about twelve when I saw a film about Thermopylae. I was so stirred that I returned to the cinema every day that week to see it again.

The story tells of the innumerable hordes of the Persian Empire who came to conquer ancient Greece. Greece was then a land of independent kingdoms, and they needed time to plan a joint defense. To buy them that time, King Leonidas of Sparta—fearless, warlike Sparta!—sped to hold off the Persian armies.

But Leonidas was not permitted to take the Spartan army. The bureaucrats saw to that, and there was no time to argue the point. So the king went with only 300 men, his personal bodyguard.

There, in the narrow pass of Thermopylae, Leonidas and three hundred Spartans stood against the Persian hordes, like a lone rock against the incoming tide. That pass was the only way into mainland Greece, so the Persians had to remove this tiny defense.

The Spartans' death was never in doubt. But it wasn't easily achieved. In the end, treachery was needed to sweep those brave men aside. By the time the Persians had won, they had lost. The Spartans had not died easily. Their courage never wavered in the face of insurmountable odds. They bought the time that Greece needed.

The might of Persia crashed upon the shores of Greece like a wave upon the rocks—and receded, broken and powerless.

As I got older, I learned that moral courage is at least as fine as physical courage. But I have never lost my admiration for physical courage. When I came across Samson, I knew I had met a marvelous hero.

Think about it:

The three hundred Spartans could at least choose their spot—the narrow pass of Thermopylae—where a few men could hold an army at bay. But Samson was brought a captive into the midst of *his* enemy.

A handful of brave RAF pilots held Hitler's war machine at bay. The heroes of the Battle of Britain were a last glorious sunset in a fading empire. Those laughing pilots with their ridiculous mustaches and ludicrous cheerfulness!—they saved the free world. But they had a weapon Hitler could not match— the Spitfire.

Samson had only a piece of bone to face a thousand well-armed soldiers.

A craven nation

After exacting justice, Samson retired out of harm's way. But the pride of the Philistines had been aroused. They couldn't catch Samson, but they knew how to capture him. A Philistine army arrived at the nearest Israelite center. The Israelites were easily awed into submission—and action. They knew where to find Samson. Three thousand of them came in order to take one brave man and hand him over to their masters.

"Do you not know," they said, "that the Philistines rule over us?" (Jud. 15:11) Samson was the only Israelite who didn't—wouldn't—know that.

Samson could never fight God's people. He extracted a promise that they wouldn't hurt him, and then submitted to be captured. Soon the Philistines saw the man they wanted, securely tied, brought into their midst.

Consider the scene:

Someone is having fun. You can hear the shouts and you see the soldiers gathered around the prisoner.

The orders were to take him back to the city to face public humiliation and death. But it seems that the prisoner is refusing to come quietly, and he will have to be killed here in the wild.

It is so frustrating! All you can see are the heads of the soldiers in front of you. What can be happening? The shouts continue, and there is the clash of steel. You would love to get closer, but so would everyone else, so you crowd forward, pressing against the men in front.

Strangely enough, you are getting closer. The ranks in front of you are thinning out. You just cannot imagine what could be going on. Over the heads in front you see a sword waving. In addition to the cries of pain, there is the sound of men panting with effort. It is as if men are fighting for their lives, but where is the enemy?

Somehow there are now only a couple of rows between you and the fight. You can see many Philistine bodies on the ground, visible between the feet of those in front. Grim-faced Philistine soldiers are facing a fearsome figure.

Can that be the Israelite prisoner? If so, he is a prisoner no more. The figure moves and spins with lightning speed. You see no weapon in his hand, but his mighty limbs are weapon enough.

Suddenly, a soldier—a comrade you know well—bursts through the ranks in front, and falls beside you. You are frozen with shock, but it is too late to help him anyway. Some terrible blow has crushed his chest, and he has died instantly.

Now only one rank lies in front of you. You can see what is happening: you can see, but you cannot believe. A terrifying figure is before you. He carries no weapon, except a piece of bone in one hand to lend deadly power to his blows.

It is as if he dances before you. He is not still for a moment. Around him are your comrades, the brave soldiers of Philistia. They crowd around, seeking an opening, ready to plunge their weapons into his body.

But he is moving with devastating speed. As he spins, his legs lash out, his fist flashes forth. He ducks and dodges, and avoids a fatal wound. But his every movement seems to send some poor soldier crashing to the ground.

Your eyes are drawn with deadly fascination to this fighting fury. He is covered with sweat and with blood, but you doubt that the blood is his own.

Then, for an instant, your eyes meet his. Those eyes are ablaze with a terrible light. You have never seen such wrath and fire before. You are chilled to the heart.

The soldier in front of you is down—it was too quick for you to see how—and you step forward to join the ring of warriors surrounding the prisoner. Everywhere your peripheral vision extends you see only the bodies of the slain. Surely this man must be exhausted from such slaughter! Now, when he is tired, he must fall. Perhaps you will be the hero who brings him down!

Soldiers lunge on the other side of the ring. The prisoner spins to avoid the blows, and fells two soldiers as he does so.

It is your chance. You aim a lightning stroke to take him in the thigh. He cannot evade your sword. He cannot—but it seems he will. His body is spinning again, turning away from your sword. But you are too fast, and you leap forward.

Time seems to slow in the midst of deadly combat. Everything is moving so slowly that it seems you can count the minutes between heartbeats.

The prisoner has moved so fast; you realize now that your sword thrust will not wound him.

You watch his hand—the hand carrying the bone—as it swings toward you. It seems, in the slowness of passing time, to be coming no faster than a leaf falling from a tree.

But it is too fast for you.

Your last sight is the prisoner's hand filling all your vision.

Your last thought is of his eyes—those terrible eyes.

The Holy Spirit tells the story thus:

> When he came to Lehi, the Philistines came shouting against him. Then the Spirit of the Lord came mightily upon him; and the ropes that were on his arms became like flax that is burned with fire, and his bonds broke loose from his hands. He found a fresh jawbone of a donkey, reached out his hand and took it, and killed a thousand men with it (Jud. 15:14-15).

Samson was brought to the Philistines bound "with two new ropes" (v. 13). New ropes would be too strong to break. How stunned they must have been to see those bonds falling from his hands!

In that moment of amazement, there was time to snatch up the nearest weapon—a donkey's jawbone. It was "fresh," and therefore not brittle. What followed is described in these words: he "killed a thousand men with it."

I have tried to picture what happened. It seems to me that Samson chose not to use a sword. Had he wanted one, he would soon have had plenty to choose from among the bodies of the dead. The sword was the premier weapon of the day, so why not use one? I suspect that it was because he had developed a different style of fighting: the "hip and thigh" method of verse 8. I imagine him kicking and punching, the archetypal martial arts exponent. The donkey's jawbone would enhance the force of his punches.

We are told that he killed the thousand men with the jawbone. I take that to mean that he used no other weapon than his own body. After a thousand were dead, the others presumably fled.

I cannot imagine that Samson had a moment's rest in the slaughter. As the Philistines fell, fresh soldiers joined the battle. They had no reason to give him an instant's respite. Even if he could take a position with his back to a rock, there must have been four or five soldiers around him at any one time. Presumably the Philistines had spears they could have thrown, so Samson could never retreat; he had to allow the mass of soldiers continually to surround him.

If Samson killed a man every twenty seconds, 180 would have died in an hour. The thousand would have taken nearly five-and-a-half hours. Just imagine those hours! Samson had to move with lightning speed to avoid the blades of his numerous opponents. And great force would be needed to kill men with kicks and punches of the jawbone, not to mention unbroken concentration and limitless stamina!

And think of his confidence! Lack of confidence loses sporting games today—and it lost battles in times past. Samson cannot have been pessimistic at the outset, or he wouldn't have lasted five minutes!

Now, think what faith you would need to face a thousand armed soldiers as Samson did! Could you trust God to give you the strength, the speed, and the concentration (your first mistake would be your last) to fight them for over five hours?

These two verses of Scripture have brought before your eyes the greatest, bravest feat of arms ever achieved. Even fiction does not dare to tell such a story! Who would believe it? But while you may indeed believe it, that is not enough. We must learn from it.

Bold or timid?

The contrast in our chapter couldn't be clearer: bold Samson, the hero of faith, and the timid Israelites.

It would be a mistake to sneer at these Israelites. They did not, I am sure, say: "We're scared of the Philistines. Let's betray Samson!" No doubt their fearfulness was rationalized into something finer.

"Discretion is the better part of valor," they might have said. "This is not a good time to fight the Philistines. Let's choose our time carefully." Maybe they rationalized their captivity. "The Philistines aren't so bad," they might have said. "At least we have a bit of law and order! The taxes aren't too bad, and we're protected from foreign invasions!"

The fact is that men find it very hard to admire cowardice. The promiscuous appear debonair; the blasphemer may seem tough. Even the thief, if he is clever, can be admired as rich and ruthless. Not so the coward: "You're afraid!" someone accuses. "I'm not!" is the instant rejoinder.

As a minister, I have found that some appeals always get a response. When we say: "Who feels they need boldness? We'll pray for them"—there are always several who do. And that's not counting those who lack the boldness to respond!

We may not be as bad as those Israelites, but are any of us

the hero that Samson was? Yet why would God have us study Samson if He was not going to increase our courage?

No sense in pretending

As a youngster I assumed that I was no coward. How could I be?—I really admired courage. But admiring something is not the same as having it. Nor is it enough to have "read the book on the subject." Before I began my training for the ministry, I spent a couple of years working with youth in London's inner city. The youth club was Christian, but the teenagers were not.

I found the youth culture of the inner city to be deprived— and violent. At one point we went through a tough period, having to call in the police several times. On one of those nights, one youngster lost his temper and kicked me in the head with steel-toed boots.

It seemed at first that I had survived the attack unscathed. Then my fellow leaders realized that I was making even less sense than usual. I had a serious concussion which lasted for several months. When I returned to the club, I was terrified. I began trembling the day before I had to be with the teenagers. They soon realized my weakness, and some took pleasure in arousing my fears. I felt utterly humiliated.

Not long after that I went to college to train as a minister. In my first months there I was filled with the Holy Spirit for the first time. It took me several years to understand what had happened, but there was no mistaking the dramatic change the Spirit had accomplished. Soon after that, I was invited back to the club to speak at a special Christmas session.

I don't know what I was expecting, but when I got there, I found it was business as usual. Someone was coming, I was told, who had sworn to kill one of the leaders. They knew him well enough to treat his threat seriously.

When he arrived, he was like a mountain. He was at least six feet tall, and very burly.

It was about time for me to begin the talk, which I did, and the "mountain" heckled me all the way through it. This proved an opportunity for the Holy Spirit to show me the difference He had made. After the talk, I was amazed to find myself going over to the "mountain" and talking to him. I had felt the Spirit prompting me to do it, but I was amazed to have obeyed! I felt no fear at all.

After a little conversation, the mountain lion became a mountain lamb. Meanwhile, elsewhere there was a fight. One of the teenage boys began beating his girlfriend's head against the wall, and she was screaming. This was the kind of thing that could lead to an all-out fight with everyone getting involved.

To my amazement I heard myself saying to the mountain lamb, "Can you sort it out?" He looked as surprised as I was. But he went over and requested that they cease. They quit fighting—immediately. As I said, he was a big guy.

What is the point of the story? It taught me that courage does not reside in me. True bravery is in God—but He will give it. However, we must know that we lack before He will fill our need.

Courage—a Christian characteristic

Classically, pagans have set a high value on courage. The great Augustine tells the tale of Mucius, a pagan Roman who tried (and failed) to kill King Porsenna, a dangerous enemy. The failed assassin was brought before the king. Did the king expect Mucius to plead for his life; to offer Roman secrets in exchange for a stay of execution?

Instead, the Roman captive "reached forth his right hand, and laid it on a red-hot altar."[1] The king watched in horror as

Mucius remarked that there were many like him, each determined to finish the job. The sight of Mucius' courage did what the Roman army could not do—King Porsenna was terrified and called off the war.

Augustine says that the courage of the Christian martyrs goes beyond even this.

You could hardly be a Christian in those first few centuries without enormous bravery. The fact was that faith in Christ could lead to torture and death. History records that Christ's friends went beyond all expectations in their valor. Far from shrinking from death, they volunteered for it. They wanted to give their dear Savior everything—more than everything. Martyrdom seemed the best way to do it.

The Roman persecution backfired. You could only watch so many Christians die in the arena before you began to despise yourself as a cowardly spectator. The dead believer lived on in your memory as a shining example of breathtaking courage. It wasn't enough that they were willing to die for their God—they sang and praised Him as they died.

The Romans queued for the arena hoping to see blood. They came out having seen the world's most eloquent visual sermons. No wonder that Tertullian observed that "the blood of the martyrs was the seed of the church." For each hero who died, many new believers sprang up from among the pagan spectators.

Cowardice and Christ do not go together

When the apostle listed those who were outside the Holy City, he put the cowardly first (Rev. 21:8). The "unbelieving, abominable, murderers, sexually immoral, sorcerers, idolaters, and all liars" come further down the list.

Jesus Himself said "Whoever denies Me before men, him I

will also deny before My Father who is in heaven" (Matt. 10:33).

Remember, cowardice is not feeling afraid—it is acting on our fear. I sometimes feel very ashamed when I think of the "great cloud of witnesses" (Heb. 12:1) that surround us. Samson is one of them, and many a martyr. They didn't hold back from following their Lord—whatever the danger.

But this is not the time to surrender to self-pity and defeat. Courage is, after all, a gift from God. No one in the apostolic era was bolder than Paul when it came to speaking for Christ. But he asked Christians to pray for him "that utterance may be given to me, that I may open my mouth boldly to make known the mystery of the Gospel" (Eph. 6:19). He knew where the boldness came from.

Learn from Peter

There is a tradition that when Peter was faced with his own martyrdom, he begged not to be crucified. Perhaps his Roman persecutors thought that the fisherman feared such a cruel death—who wouldn't? But it turned out that Peter felt that he wasn't worthy to share the same death as his Savior. He was crucified upside down at his own request. It's a brave man who can only think of his own unworthiness when his martyrdom is impending. Was Peter always so brave?

He used to think he was.

Peter told Jesus, "Even if I have to die with You, I will not deny you!" (Matt 26:35). This was during the Last Supper. It seemed no idle boast: in the garden, it was Peter who defended Jesus with his sword (John 18:10). Then, when the others had fled, Peter followed Jesus into the lions' den—the High Priest's palace.

Did Peter plan some sort of brave rescue attempt? I suspect so. He tried to disguise his identity, and was waiting for his moment.

Then, to his horror, he saw Jesus looking at him (Luke 22:61). The cock had crowed, and Peter had just been pretending to be no disciple. We are told that "Peter went out and wept bitterly" (v. 62).

What was he supposed to do—get himself crucified? Well, yes, he was.

This is the time to share Peter's bitter tears. What do you think of the courage you have heard of in this chapter? Does Samson put us to shame? How about the Christless Leonidas and Mucius—or the innumerable heroes of the Roman arena?

Peter might have defended himself: "I was going to rescue Jesus—I could hardly admit I was a disciple!" And we could defend ourselves too. All those times when we were silent, when we could have spoken; the times we refused to stand out from the crowd. How important has it been for us to avoid the anguish of rejection and persecution? "Woe to you when all men speak well of you," says Jesus, "for so did their fathers to the false prophets" (Luke 6:26).

Why pretend? It is far better for us to face our weaknesses. We are not what we should be—yet.

Peter's longest swim

Peter never saw Jesus again before His crucifixion. Imagine how he felt: Jesus is tortured, condemned, crucified—and Peter is in hiding. There was nothing to do but think about his cowardice and failure. And there the story would have ended had Jesus stayed dead. But it wasn't the end for Peter, and it isn't for us either.

After the Resurrection, Peter and the others are earning their daily bread again. They are fishing, and a stranger calls from the shore. Soon they recognize Him: "It is the Lord!" cries John (John 21:7). John starts bringing the boat to shore, but Peter has never been very good at delays.

He plunges into the sea. It is only a short swim to Jesus, but it must have seemed so long to this sad man. Here is Jesus—his friend; Jesus—whom he denied. Peter busies himself dragging the fish to shore, and then they are sharing a breakfast Jesus has prepared.

After breakfast, Jesus wants words with Peter. "Here it comes," Peter must have thought. "I deserve whatever He says." Peter has ruined his future as an apostle.

Jesus has a question for His friend. "Do you love Me?" He asks (John 21:15-17). Yes, Peter does. But it seems He is not convinced. Jesus repeats the question. Peter becomes sad at this point (v. 17). What is Jesus saying? Presumably Jesus doubts Peter's love, and has no more use for him. But it is not so. Peter is to look after Jesus' sheep. After his awful failure, Peter must have been speechless with joy to be given such an enormous commission.

The bad news—or is it really the good news?—is that he will "glorify God" by a martyr's death (vv. 18-19). If the old tradition is true, we know how Peter viewed this news. It was good news, albeit too good for him in his own estimation.

We too need to see Jesus about our cowardice. It isn't an easy thing to do because we fear rejection. But I believe that we will be amazed at what Jesus has to say to us. I believe that we will find that "the one who comes to me I will by no means cast out" (John 6:37).

Bold witnesses in a humanistic world

This is what Jesus said:

> Whatever I tell you in the dark, speak in the light; and what you hear in the ear, preach on the housetops. And do not fear those who kill the body but cannot kill the soul. But rather fear him

who is able to destroy both soul and body in hell. Are not two sparrows sold for a copper coin? And not one of them falls to the ground apart from your Father's will. But the very hairs of your head are all numbered. Do not fear therefore; you are of more value than many sparrows. Therefore whoever confesses Me before men, him I will also confess before My Father who is in heaven (Matt. 10:27-32).

Unlike imperial Rome, Western humanists have no prisons and torture for Christians. Conversion doesn't point us to the dungeon and the arena. But, for all that, we have great need of boldness. The gentleness of the humanist, like that of the Philistine, keeps most of us fairly quiet. We could speak, but somehow we don't as much as we should.

But Jesus calls us to be courageous like Samson, rather than acquiescent like his countrymen. Our friends and neighbors are unlikely to find the way to heaven unless we tell them, or at least bring them where they can hear. Like Peter, we must set ourselves to "preach on the housetops."

John the Baptist died because of his testimony. What part of his testimony proved so fatal? John had declared that King Herod's marriage, although legal, was unlawful in God's eyes (Mark 6:17-18). Herod imprisoned him; his wife grasped the opportunity and the prophet's head was dished up on a plate (vv. 19-28).

Had John stayed out of politics he would perhaps have lived longer. Longer, but not better. John, like Samson a life-long Nazirite, refused to confine his testimony within acceptable limits. If something was wrong, John would say so, whatever the legalities.

How about us? Have we the courage to speak out on unpopular issues? Shall we be bold in the face of furious opposition?

Where the law of the land is unlawful in God's eyes, are we prepared to say so?

The early church faced the abortion issue just like we do today. Listen to what Basil, one great leader, wrote:

> The woman who purposely destroys her unborn child is guilty of murder. . . . Women also who administer drugs to cause abortion, as well as those who take poisons to destroy unborn children, are murderesses.[2]

Such a statement sounds harsh in our ears, but Basil was not a harsh man. He loved God, who forbids murder, and especially the killing of unborn children (Ex. 21:22-23). He pitied the children so cruelly killed before they were even born. He cared for the souls of these women, and wanted to save them from incurring awful guilt.

No doubt we share his love for God and for people. But do we share his boldness, his willingness to speak without fear? The love and firmness of the early church brought an end to abortion for many centuries. Yes, they saw a wonderful revival, right across (and beyond) the Roman world. The whole of society was changed, much good and happiness resulted.

But none of it would have happened if the Christians had kept their mouths shut.

The needs of our age are urgent. We must speak. Each of us must be a Samson, insisting on doing God's will whatever the opposition.

---

1. Augustine's *City of God*, Book 5, Chapter 18. Schaff's edition of *The Nicene and Post-Nicene Fathers*, first series, vol. 2 (reprinted by Hendrickson Publishers, Inc., 1994), 99.
2. Basil in *The Nicene and Post-Nicene Fathers*, Second Series, vol. 8 (reprinted by

THE PRAYER OF FAITH

Judges 15:16-20

Suddenly, the soldiers were gone. Samson looked up and found that he had won. A thousand lay dead at his feet—the rest were fleeing for their lives. His mind, quick with riddles, was quick with rhyme too. A catchy lyric leapt from his lips:

> With the jawbone of a donkey,
> Heaps upon heaps,
> With the jawbone of a donkey
> I have slain a thousand men! (Jud. 15:16)

This may not sound particularly catchy to us, but it is much better in the original Hebrew. Surprisingly, the words for "donkey" and "heap" here are the same. If Samson had used a piece of a chimney stack instead of jawbone, I could convey the pun like this:

> With a chimney stack,
> Stacks and stacks!
> With a chimney stack,
> A thousand I hacked!

"Was this really a time for poetry?" you may ask. But Samson was already looking beyond this victory to the next. As we know, victory in hand-to-hand combat—as with sport—depends partly on the morale of the soldiers. Samson had killed a thousand Philistines; now he would destroy the morale of the rest. He flings the jawbone in a fine gesture of contempt at the fleeing Philistines. He renames the region "Ramath Lehi"—"Jawbone Hill."

What effect do you think this would have had on the Philistines? Jawbone Hill soon had its own water supply, and would have been a good place to take the sheep.

"Can you tell me," someone asks, "the way to Jawbone Hill?"

"Away with you!" growls the Philistine in reply. Just hearing the new name would remind them of their worst humiliation. I imagine that Samson's verse soon had a tune. I imagine too that the Philistines became quite familiar with it. I should think even hearing it being whistled would have done the trick.

What happened next?

Actually, nothing happened next. Samson's song may have been on every Israelite's lips; Jawbone Hill was on all the maps; but Samson still had the monopoly on Israelite courage.

We know what the Philistines would have done because in David's day it was they who had the unbeatable champion. Goliath was a giant whom nobody dare face in combat (see 1 Sam. 17). At that time, the Philistines invaded, and drew out the Israelite army. Then when the armies were face-to-face, Goliath stepped out and challenged anyone to single combat. Of course, nobody wanted to fight him. So time passed with Philistine morale rising and Israelite morale falling, until a shepherd boy visited the camp.

No doubt the Philistines were expecting Samson at the head of an Israelite army. Who would want to face him in single combat?

But nothing happened.

Why was this? Was Samson unwilling to act? I doubt that.

It must therefore have been the Israelites. Once again, they chose to stay under the Philistine yoke. But then how could they be ready for victory? They still had their idols (1 Sam. 7:3). And although discouraged, the Philistines were still very strong. Samson had dealt their morale a terrible blow, but they still had their leaders. To destroy their morale completely, he would have had to destroy their officers, and how could anyone do that?

Are you sick of hearing about the cowardly Israelites? If so, come with me back to Samson, who will cap his heroic feat with a stand of wonderful moral courage.

Meanwhile, back at Jawbone Hill

Verse sung and jawbone flung, Samson sinks to the ground. Hours of amazing effort have left him dehydrated. If he had a few flesh wounds, the dehydration would have been even worse.

He has been brought to the point of death. He *must* drink. Without a miracle, he will die.

And yet, he is surrounded by water. There is water in the waterskins of the dead Philistine soldiers. In those days, people knew water to be a vital commodity. They could not turn on the tap when they were thirsty. Cities might have cisterns, but otherwise you would have to go and fetch your water from the well.

People can easily die of thirst in a hot climate. Soldiers, therefore, would travel with their own water supply. Of course they would, otherwise the thirst would kill them if there was no water near the battlefield. Soldiers have always carried water in bottles or skins on their belts. This is far better than pulling along some traveling water tank. Such a water tank would be cumbersome and an easy target for the enemy. And it's easier to ration water if everyone has their own private supply.

So, we may take it as certain that these Philistine soldiers had brought their own water. They had encamped in Judah (Jud. 15:9) and threatened the locals. They had to be ready to fight.

That means there were a thousand waterskins, attached to the thousand corpses at Samson's feet.

Why a miracle?

So why didn't Samson just empty a couple of waterskins? The answer is: his Nazirite vow prohibited him. A Nazirite "shall not go near a dead body" (Num. 6:6). Probably the waterskins were fastened around the soldiers' waists. Samson would have had to approach a corpse, move the body to undo the belt, and then disentangle the waterskin.

Rather than break his vow, Samson was prepared to die. I think this a remarkable act of moral courage.

David found himself in a similar situation. We read that he had to escape from King Saul, and he and his followers were hungry. He went into the holy place, and ate the showbread, "which was not lawful for him to eat, nor for those who were with him, but only for the priests" (Matt. 12:4).

Did he do wrong then? Jesus said not (see Matt. 12:1-8) because these ritual laws gave way before the life-and-death situation David faced.

On that basis, Samson could have taken water from the dead Philistines, and not sinned. But he wouldn't. He wanted to be the very best he could be for his God.

Samson prayed a desperate prayer. "Shall I die of thirst?" he asked. In answer, "God split the hollow place that is in Lehi, and water came out, and he drank; and his spirit returned, and he revived" (Jud. 15:19). This was no momentary miracle. There had been no water in that place; now there was a spring. He called the spring "En Hakkore" ("Spring of the Caller"), because he had called on God for it. Fifteen centuries later, in Jerome's time (fourth century), this spring was still well known.

It was a remarkable answer to prayer. We have much to learn from Samson.

God answers His people's prayers

Jesus encourages us to pray, and not to give up. He promises to answer our prayers. Of course every Christian knows this. We are familiar with such texts as these:

> Ask, and it will be given to you; seek, and you will find; knock, and it will be opened to you. For everyone who asks receives, and he who seeks finds, and to him who knocks it will be opened (Matt. 7:7-8).

> And whatever you ask in My name, that I will do, that the Father may be glorified in the Son. If you ask anything in My name, I will do it (John 14:13-14).

In practice though we are sometimes unsure about whether God will answer our prayers. Have we ever asked for anything remotely as big as Samson did here? Asking for water in a desert seems as hard as moving mountains! What have we asked for? A friend to become a Christian? Money to pay a bill? Protection for a child?

And when we asked, did we expect our prayer to be answered? I think that many of us nurse a secret uncertainty about prayer. As new Christians we prayed with an optimistic, childlike faith. A few years later, "reality" has battered us, and we pray with less confidence.

When His friends were full of unbelief at Lazarus' tomb, Jesus said: "Did I not say to you that if you would believe you would see the glory of God?" (John 11:40) Then He answered their prayer with an amazing display of His power. Samson saw the glory of God in answer to his prayer. Let's see how he prayed.

Samson glorified God by obedience

We have seen how Samson preferred to die rather than drink the water the dead Philistines carried. How determined he must have been to obey God to the fullest!

It seems to me that Samson's uppermost thought was to deliver Israel. When the battle was over, he made up that catchy, morale-boosting verse. A man exhausted—about to die from dehydration—does not amuse himself composing ditties. I think that Samson was so committed to rousing Israel that he turned his mind immediately to using his victory as a benefit for his people.

Others may have said: "I've done enough for today! I'll worry about Israel tomorrow!" Not Samson—like Jesus, who thought of His mother's needs while on the cross (John 19:26-27)—He considered Israel. This is so important! Jesus, when He taught about the "faith to move mountains," added: "And whenever you stand praying, if you have anything against anyone, forgive him" (Mark 11:25). This was not a new topic, but a vital part of the truth about prayer. Answered prayer and harmony among believers go together.

The same God who answers our prayers commands our lives. And He commands us to live in love and harmony with each other. "Again I say to you that if two of you agree on earth," Jesus said, "concerning anything that they ask, it will be done for them by My Father in heaven" (Matt. 18:19).

Why are obedience and answered prayer so bound together? The reason is that prayer is our cooperating with God to achieve His ends. Yes, He does want to bless us, to "give us the desires of our heart" (Ps. 37:4). But that is part of a bigger picture: God has His perfect plans.

That's why David says: "If I regard iniquity in my heart, the Lord will not hear" (Ps. 66:18). In the matter of Delilah, Samson did regard iniquity in his heart. When the Philistines came for him, God did not hear him. The apostle states the principle thus:

Whatever we ask we receive from Him, because
we keep His commandments and do those things
that are pleasing in His sight (1 John 3:22).

"Because we keep His commandments"? That sounds as if
we earn answers to our prayers. Not at all—it is a matter of
truth, of being consistent. If I pray, I am seeking to be part of
God's aims. If I disobey Him, I am working against God's aims.

It wouldn't be kindness on God's part to allow me to be so
inconsistent. It is good for me to see things as they are. It is no
good praying for the money to pay that bill if I don't also pray for
grace to keep my temper. In any case, there is something at stake
far more important than what is good for me.

All this brings a remarkable story to mind. I was at the front
of a large Christian gathering, bringing the meeting to a close.
The Word had been preached, and there was a sense that "the
power of the Lord was present" (Luke 5:17).

Standing there, I was prompted to say that I thought there
were believers present who needed to put things right with one
another; to apologize, to forgive. I invited people to come forward as a means of saying "yes" to the Lord. It isn't easy to
respond to an invitation of this sort. By standing up, and strid-
ing forward, you are telling everyone that you have been nursing
a grudge against someone. It takes some courage. On that occasion, dozens had the courage.

As they prayed at the front, I had another prompting. "I
believe," I said, "that God wants to heal someone whose ailment is
in the lower back and left leg. I believe too that you must put something right first. If that is you—come forward and I'll pray for you."

I waited for someone to come forward, but actually someone
came back. A girl in a wheelchair was returning to her place. She
had come to the front earlier to commit herself to forgive and
apologize.

"I have already put that something right!" she said, her face wreathed in smiles. Her ailment had kept her in a wheelchair for the last year. We prayed. God began to heal her immediately. By the next day, she was able to sing and dance in worship to the Lord.

She glorified God in obedience. She had been praying for the healing of this specific ailment for the last year, but God chose that moment to answer those prayers.

Samson gave God the glory

Samson has just won the most heroic victory of all time. He has, as his verse says, "slain a thousand men." How does he view this mighty feat?

"You have given this great deliverance," he says, "by the hand of Your servant" (Jud. 15:18). He gives God the glory for this great victory.

This may seem the obvious, the only sensible view. But we are not always sensible. We find it all too easy to congratulate ourselves on what God has done in us. The apostle has to ask: "Who makes you differ from another? And what do you have that you did not receive? Now if you did indeed receive it, why do you boast as if you had not received it?" (1 Cor. 4:7)

Which of us has not prayed humbly for something, and then been proud of it when it was given?

The Holy Spirit warns us that "pride goes before destruction, and a haughty spirit before a fall" (Prov. 16:18). This is as sure as the law of gravity: "What goes up must come down" is as true of human pride as it is of footballs. God says: "My glory I will not give to another" (Isa. 42:8). This isn't because He is mean or selfish, but because He is Truth. He really is the source and center of all life. His is the glory, whatever anyone thinks. So, to allow us to take the glory, to revolve the universe around our petty selves, would not be right.

When pride takes us, the subsequent fall is a (hidden) blessing. Faces flat on the floor, we see the situation from a more realistic viewpoint. So it would be no kindness to answer our prayers if that simply reinforced our pride.

Samson could attribute his wonderful heroism to God, and we can emulate him.

Many years ago, when I was a young minister, I visited an old lady from my church. She came to all the church meetings, but I hardly knew her. She was so quiet and inconspicuous. We sat, and she told me her troubles. Clearly the answer was prayer.

I asked her if she knew much about prayer, and her answer confirmed my suspicions. She looked with humble admiration at the young minister before her. "I don't really know how to pray properly," she said.

"Well, do you ever try? What do you pray?" I asked. I had so much to teach her, but where to start?

"Well, I don't know," she said. "I just close my eyes, and open my hands like this." She showed me how she did it. I watched with superior indulgence.

"Then," she said, "I feel Jesus take my hands. He holds my hands, and I just talk to Him."

I was aghast. What could I say? I had been rendered speechless (a rare experience for me). Not familiar with humility, I had entirely misread the spiritual giant before me.

All she did was hold Jesus' hands, and talk to Him? Her prayer times were a continuous miracle! I wished—and still wish—I knew a fraction of what she knew. I had been ready to teach her clever techniques and lessons, but it seemed that Jesus preferred her humility to all my expertise (see Isa. 57:15; 66:2).

Samson sought God's glory

Why should God have answered Samson's prayer? Samson thanks God for his victory and asks "Now shall I die of thirst and fall into the hand of the uncircumcised?" (Jud. 15:18)

The "uncircumcised" are the Philistines. Why did Samson use that word? It is to highlight the vital issue: who is on God's side? The first step of obedience under the Old Covenant was circumcision. The Philistines had not taken that first step.

The point is not that Samson deserves to be rescued. He doesn't say: "Save me, I've been a good Nazirite; I've always done Your will." He says: "Don't let those who disobey You be the winners!" In other words: "You win, Lord!"

As we saw earlier, the point of prayer is that we cooperate with God's plan, not that He submits to ours. This suits us well, because His plan for us is far better than anything we could have devised. But, of course, need and desire send us to God, begging that He do our will. This is not what God has promised!

Now this is the confidence that we have in Him, that if we ask anything according to His will, He hears us (1 John 5:14).

Jesus—fully a man—felt the awful intensity of human need. The terrible torture of Calvary set Him praying for deliverance. "O my Father," He begged, "if it is possible, let this cup pass from Me" (Matt. 26:39). But He didn't end there. "Nevertheless," He added, "not as I will, but as You will."

We should always pray for what we believe is God's will. Of course, it is right to "be anxious for nothing, but in everything by prayer and supplication, with thanksgiving, let your requests be made known to God" (Phil. 4:6). We tell Him what we think we need. And we hang on to His promises. But if things don't work out as we wished, He didn't break His word. He does the best thing, whether we recognize it or not. That's why we let our requests be made known to God—with thanksgiving.

Righteous Job saw his life crumble, and his prayers all apparently unanswered. He became desperately unhappy.

Naked I came from my mother's womb,
And naked shall I return there.

> The Lord gave, and the Lord has taken away;
> Blessed be the name of the Lord (Job 1:21).

As their sorrows increased, his wife became impatient with his faith in God.

> His wife said to him, "Do you still hold fast to your integrity? Curse God and die!" But he said to her, "You speak as one of the foolish women speaks. Shall we indeed accept good from God, and shall we not accept adversity?" (Job 2:9-10)

The days will come when you and I will find eternity too short to thank God enough for His matchless grace. We shall see what now we must accept by faith.

"We know that all things work together for good to those who love God, to those who are the called according to His purpose" (Rom. 8:28). We know it now, by faith. One day we will see. "I shall know just as I also am known" (1 Cor. 13:12). Yes, eternity will be too short to thank Him. Obviously we should get busy with it now.

This is the truth. Don't let apparently unanswered prayer discourage you. The apostle had already said, "We do not know what we should pray for as we ought" (Rom. 8:26)—now he guarantees that God always knows how to answer our prayers, making "all things work together for good."

I have a friend whose wife left him. He really loved her, and would never have believed that she might be unfaithful. Then, one day, she announced that she had a lover; she was leaving. She and her lover had everything organized: where they were going to live, what would happen to the children.

That day, he prayed as he had never prayed before. "If You only answer one prayer of mine, Lord," he pleaded, "let this be the one." Then there came a ray of hope. His wife's Christian commitment fought against her continuing in adultery. He prayed all the harder, and began to hope that God would work the miracle.

But in the end, her choice fell on the adultery.

"Where were You, Lord?" he complained in his anguish. It seemed that God had answered many smaller prayers, but had let him down when it really mattered.

But the story didn't end there. A few years later, my friend had a very different view of the matter.

His wife had broken the marriage and he was left a single man. Then God had brought someone new into his life. They had fallen in love, and were now married. From his new vantagepoint, my friend realized how unhappy he had been with his first wife. Loving her had blinded him to how hard she had made his life. Now remarried, he felt truly loved for the first time. His whole life began to blossom; he felt happier than he could have believed possible.

So—what about the unanswered prayer?

"I thank God," he says, "for *not* answering my prayer!"

But, actually, God did answer his prayer—not to the letter, but better. Faced with his wife's adultery, he had begged that God would make her faithful again. In the end, God gave him a wife who was truly faithful. Not merely was she not an adulteress, but she really kept faith with her marriage commitment—she really loved him, and set out to make him happy.

Who knows what the future holds? Who knows if people's sin will be used to our benefit? My friend is glad that he prayed as he did. It was right to do everything he could to save the marriage. But he has learned not to criticize God when He doesn't answer prayers in the way we want.

The next twenty years

When we hear of Samson next, twenty years have passed. What happened in those twenty years? Samson, we are told, judged Israel (Jud. 15:20) through that time. So there was Samson, hearing the disputes of the people, and resolving them by the law of God. How was it with his soul? Not good, it seems, as we shall see.

By the time the twenty years are over, we find Samson strangely weakened in his obedience before God. We shall see why that was. Meanwhile, other forces were at work preparing Israel for their moment of transformation.

The ark of the covenant

We left the story of the ark with its return from Philistine captivity. We saw how the Israelites at Beth Shemesh had been punished by God for their blasphemous curiosity (see 1 Sam. 6:19). After that, the ark was moved to Kiriath Jearim, near Samson's base. It stayed there for the twenty years of Samson's rule. Meanwhile, the tabernacle where it had been housed remained at Shiloh. During that time, we are told, "all the house of Israel lamented after the Lord" (1 Sam. 7:2).

Why were they so sad? It was because they felt they were in disgrace. The ark could not be restored to the tabernacle at Shiloh. The ark and the priestly center remained separate until Solomon built the temple. Why was this? Perhaps because God renews what sin ruins, rather than patching things up. Solomon's temple brought in a glorious new era for Israel. Things were never quite satisfactory before that.

Clearly Israel realized how unsatisfactory things were over those twenty years. They were still under Philistine rule. The ark—the symbol of God's presence in their midst—was away from the holy place.

Jephthah's daughter

We saw earlier that the Philistines had taken over the west of Israel. The east had been conquered by the Ammonites (Jud. 10:6). Jephthah was the judge whom God used to rescue the eastern part of Israel. Before his great victory, Jephthah had promised to make a sacrifice to God if he were given victory. The sacrifice was to be "whatever comes out of the doors of my house to meet me, when I return in peace from the people of Ammon" (Jud. 11:31).

Jephthah did indeed win the battle. But to his distress, it was his daughter who came out to greet him on his return. She was his only child (v. 34), but he would not retract his vow.

Obviously human sacrifice was out of the question (Deut. 12:31). In such cases a financial offering could be given in place of the person (Lev. 27:1-8). But it seems that Jephthah's daughter was dedicated to the house of God, as Samuel had been (1 Sam. 1:22, 28).

To be dedicated fully to the service of God, this woman had to remain single. Years later, the apostle said: "The unmarried woman cares about the things of the Lord, that she may be holy both in body and in spirit. But she who is married cares about the things of the world—how she may please her husband" (1 Cor. 7:34). Not only would she never know romantic love, she would be childless. This must have weighed heavily on Jephthah because his line would end with her.

Jephthah's daughter was clearly a very fine person. She encouraged her father to keep his vow. But it was very hard on her. "Let me alone for two months," she begged, "that I may go and wander on the mountains and bewail my virginity, my friends and I" (Jud. 11:37). Her father granted her request. After that, she returned and entered into her vow. "She knew no man," we are told (v. 39).

I imagine her lifelong ministry as similar to that of Anna: she "did not depart from the temple, but served God with fastings and prayers night and day" (Luke 2:37). Her name is not remembered, but her godly example made a great impact. "It became a custom in Israel," we are told, "that the daughters of Israel went four days each year to lament the daughter of Jephthah" (vv. 39-40).

Why did they "lament" her? Actually this word "lament" (in Hebrew, *tanah*) comes in only one other place in Scripture, in Judges 5:11. There it is translated "recount"—"they shall recount the righteous acts of the Lord." "Praise" is the best translation; *tanah* does not mean to lament or bewail, but to praise.[1]

"Praise" fits well with the context. I picture these women admiring her life of prayer and dedication. They "praised" her commitment. They were full of admiration for her intimacy with God. Unlike Samuel, she seems never to have played a public role in Israel. But imagine that annual celebration! Imagine women coming to visit her, and seeing a life of dedicated prayer.

"I wish I could be like her!" some would have said. They praised her—and her example of prayerfulness would work its way into the minds of the people.

The twenty years passed. God was moving Israel closer and closer to the moment when they would repent, find their courage, and return to the Lord.

Samuel played his part, Jephthah's daughter played hers. Samson was still undefeated, and events would soon hasten to their dramatic conclusion.

---

1. Keil on Judges, Keil & Delitzsch's *Old Testament Commentary*, "Judges" (reprinted by Eerdmans, 1976), 388.

9 TWENTY YEARS ON

Judges 16:1-3

The first thing she looks for is the eyes. She knows how to read a man's eyes. Some say they are the window of the soul; but such profundities are of little interest to her.

She just needs to know why a man visits her. Does he represent law and order? Has he come on behalf of a sister, jealous of her husband?

Or has he come for her with money in his pocket?

The eyes tell it all.

She looks at the stranger's eyes and finds the desire she is looking for. Where there is that look, the money is always at hand. And whatever she may tell her customers, it is the money she really desires.

Shame and awkwardness hood those eyes. But that is all right with her. Men come to her, betraying wives, covering their visits with lies. Not many are proud of themselves. It has been a long time since she wondered if she is proud of herself. What does it matter, so long as the men have brought their money?

But at this man she spares a second glance. Can it be who she thinks it is?

"And what can I do for you?" she inquires, as she wonders whether to admit him.

"You know," replies his gruff voice. His hand jingles the sound of money. But his accent, plus that unforgettable face, has given him away. She knows who the stranger is at her door. She doesn't know whether she should run or stay. Is the conqueror of armies here in Gaza to humiliate her people again? Or is the judge of Israel about to sample the pleasures of Philistine life?

Is he here to teach me a lesson? she wonders. *Or has he come to learn one?*

She knows men—or at least a certain kind of man. And as she looks at the stranger, she begins to realize that he is just that kind of man. She steps aside and allows him to enter. Soon she will find a way to alert her people. They will be very interested to know who her guest is. Not just interested, but grateful too, she hopes.

She hopes the stranger will enjoy his last night. It will cost him a lot more than he thinks.

If the prostitute was surprised, we are astonished. It is hard to believe that this is the great hero of faith we have come to know. This is the man who never shrank from danger. Whether ravenous lion or battle-hardened soldiers, none ever saw his back. God made him so strong! He alone stood when the fighting finished.

His wisdom had the Philistines racking their brains to answer a riddle. He knew how to set fire to Philistine fields—however many firefighters fought the flames.

He would rather die than take water from a dead soldier.

His greatness dwarfs us—and now he is under a prostitute's roof? What has happened in these last twenty years?

Eroded grandeur

We are told no details, but it isn't hard to imagine what might have happened. The passage of time would have brought little joy to Samson. Israel was still unchanged—cowardly and idolatrous. He was to see their cowardice soon enough when he removed Gaza's main defense, her gates, and Israel took no advantage of it!

As judge, Samson would be hearing the same sort of cases over and over again. How depressing it must have been! What a daily reminder that Israel was as far as ever from deliverance! A man will press through the discouragements if he can see his goal drawing closer. But how hard it must have been for Samson! Why hadn't they risen from their captivity after his last great victory? What more could he do? How could he rouse Israel?

Had he failed?

No one had ever stood with Samson. His strength had seen him through. But what would time do to his strength? Aged now around forty, Samson realized that he too must grow old. Soon his strength must wane. How long before the Philistines would take him?

In times of discouragement, a man longs for solace. But where was there solace for the hero? His Nazirite vow denied him the consolation that others enjoyed. "Give strong drink to him who is perishing," says the Scripture, "and wine to those who are bitter of heart" (Prov. 31:6).

There is great consolation in the family. We saw how the Nazirite vow denied him some of that consolation. His uncut hair kept Samson different from everyone else. It separated him from people. How hard that is for a man who is longing for reassurance!

Not good for a man to be alone

Scripture speaks of a gift of celibacy (1 Cor. 7:7). The Apostle Paul had it, but Samson didn't. Without that gift "it is better to marry than burn with passion" (v. 9). There is no shame in "burning"—God gave the passion, however much the Devil would like people to think it his invention.

Samson had burned—and married. We have seen how soon his wife was taken away. But clearly he still burned. So why had he not remarried?

The answer, I suspect, lies in his lifestyle. The Philistines would dearly have loved to get their hands on Samson. We shall see the Philistines of Gaza going to great lengths to capture him (Jud. 16:2). Clearly, Samson could not risk living a settled life. The whereabouts of his home would soon be known. Then it would only be a matter of time before the Philistines came for him. He would never know when he would be awakened by naked blades and sudden death.

Even if Samson could bear that, what woman could? So Samson remained unmarried. It must have been so very hard.

Meanwhile, Israel was still in its idolatry. The Scriptures show us how idolatry and adultery usually go together. As a judge, Samson would soon become aware of how easily people indulged in sexual sin. As a judge, Samson punished the adulterous. But as a man, he longed for physical solace himself.

We cannot excuse Samson, but perhaps we can understand him.

Samson in Gaza

Why find a prostitute in Gaza? If Samson were to indulge in sexual sin, he had several options. Adultery is the most serious of sexual sins, worthy of death. How could a judge become an adulterer? But neither did he seek out an unmarried woman, perhaps because he didn't want to set a young person on the wrong track.

In fact, Samson committed his sin in Philistine territory. Perhaps he thought that they were already on the wrong track—a prostitute more than any. I suspect that when he decided to sin, he chose the setting in which he would do the least harm. This does nothing to excuse the inexcusable, but it may have been the way he reasoned.

No doubt Samson hoped to remain unrecognized—just another Israelite sampling pagan pleasures in a pagan town. God saw to it that he was recognized. The Philistines shut the main gate and waited for daylight. Gaza was a fortified town. That means that walls surrounded it, and only the main gate allowed access. Once the gate was closed there was no getting out. The gates were the weakest part of the wall. For that reason such gates were strong and heavy. Clearly no one could just pick them up and walk off with them.

But this is precisely what Samson did. I can picture the Philistines waking up to see their town utterly unprotected! Where the gates should be there was nothing, not even the gateposts! They would have looked for some clue as to what had happened. Since Samson had carried an enormous weight, his feet must have left *very* deep footprints. I can see the Philistines following these footprints, right up a hill, and seeing the gates just lying there. Someone kneels down and measures just how deep the footprints are. Nobody likes what they are seeing.

When Israel gets 'round to throwing off their yoke, city gates are not going to stop them. They'll just send in Samson, and he'll remove them.

Samson's eyes
"Samson went to Gaza and saw a harlot there" (Jud. 16:1). This

reminds us of twenty years before: "Samson saw a woman in Timnah" (Jud. 14:1). The wise man says: "Charm is deceitful and beauty is passing" (Prov. 31:30). We are to look for the inner beauty of the soul—not mere outward appearances—unless we wish our hearts to be broken.

But Samson's wife had broken his heart. And now his eyes were in charge again.

A blind man once told me that adultery is very uncommon among the blind. The Holy Spirit warns us against the "lust of the eyes" (1 John 2:16). There is no doubt that as we gaze at the forbidden thing, its attraction grows. It wasn't until Eve gave the tree a second glance that she decided "that it was pleasant to the eyes, and a tree desirable" (Gen. 3:6). After that, "she took of its fruit and ate."

There is a progression in temptation. First, someone is "drawn away by his own desires and enticed" (James 1:14). This deceptive enticement is the tiny seed that grows to greater things. "When desire has conceived, it gives birth to sin; and sin, when it is full-grown, brings forth death" (v. 15). So, the crucial battle is at the beginning. Yes, while danger feels so distant, when the soul seems so secure, a deadly seed is planted.

Sin is against God's interests, and it is against ours too. It destroys us. Its primary strategy, therefore, must be to deceive us. The apostle warns us, "lest any of you be hardened through the deceitfulness of sin" (Heb. 3:13). Sin must disguise itself as something good for us, a stolen pleasure, a benefit. However, once our minds have been enlightened by God, we become aware of the realities of life. We know that sin is bad for us.

So temptation tries to bypass the mind. The *eyes* see the forbidden thing, and temptation adds the fantasies of pleasure and fulfillment. Thus it must have been with Samson. He knew he was damaging himself, but his flesh wouldn't allow him to attend to what he knew.

This was the moment to cry out to God, to "subdue our iniquities" (Micah 7:19)—but Samson didn't. I imagine that he repented once he realized that God was punishing him. He knew he would need supernatural strength to escape from Gaza, and I don't think God would have helped him, had he been planning to continue with the sin. But I suspect that the repentance didn't go deep enough. Sin's grip was soon reasserted, as we shall see when Delilah comes on the scene.

But how could this man of faith have fallen so easily? How could his greatness so easily have disappeared?

Weakened by strength

The very things that made Samson strong, also made him weak.

Imagine what it would have been like to be Samson. God called him to be different, and different he certainly was. As Samson mixed with others, his Nazirite vow set him apart. He certainly wasn't one of the crowd. His distinctiveness invited comparisons. Did others have high aims, noble ambitions? He more so because God Himself had given Samson his life's aim.

When it came to courage, strength, and many other virtues, Samson surpassed everyone. But he wasn't just muscle and heroism. He was wise, clever, and resourceful. He was even a verse maker, with a number-one hit—his "Donkey's Jawbone" song!

Did others pray? When Samson prayed, a miraculous spring appeared! His prayer had changed the landscape! It wasn't that Samson thought himself more gifted than others—he really was! And these wonderful gifts had come so early in his life. He had never known crushing failure; he had never had to strive and endure defeat to reach a goal.

The point is this: Samson's strengths must have made him feel strong, inherently strong. That is why he had only learned half the secret of strength in all his exploits up to this point. He had not reached the stage where he could agree that "when I am weak, then I am strong" (2 Cor. 12:10).

But why should his strength have led to his fall into sin?

The essence of sin

Augustine said that pride was the basis of all sin; Luther thought it was unbelief. Actually, these two great masters of the Word agree, because pride and unbelief come to the same thing. God says that "He will beautify the humble with salvation" (Ps. 149:4). Elsewhere, He says that He saves those who believe (John 3:16). So which is it? Is it the humble or those with faith who are saved?

The answer is that you can't have one without the other. Sin is a lack of both. This becomes clear as we look at the first sin.

Adam and Eve found themselves in a paradise not of their own making. Wherever they looked, they saw beauty and loveliness. And it was clear that they had God to thank for it all. He made them and everything around them. When the tempter came, it was to point them to the one thing forbidden—the tree of the knowledge of good and evil. Why should they want to eat this fruit?

It was that "you will be like God, knowing good and evil" (Gen. 3:5). The "knowledge" the tree represented was the godlike, "deciding for oneself what is right." This is called "autonomy"—when I formulate my own morality, without God. It is the morality of humanism. By taking the fruit, Adam and Eve chose to direct their own lives.

Once fallen, mankind had lost everything that really matters. All men had was their claim to a godlike control over their own lives. They still know what is right and what is wrong—in their own eyes. They don't need God to tell them how to live. Miserable, lost, destined for endless anguish—the humanist is still his own god.

God's way of life

The shock of mankind's fall was still reverberating in the air when God spoke a promise that shaped the whole of future history. He told the Devil:

> I will put enmity
> Between you and the woman,
> And between your seed and her seed;
> he shall bruise your head,
> And you shall bruise his heel (Gen. 3:15).

Christ was the promised "seed" who would overcome the enemy, at great personal cost. This was mankind's only hope. However mysterious the promise seemed, one thing was very clear. Man's only hope lay outside himself. He could not save himself. He would never be his own savior.

He had usurped the very throne of God, to his own appalling cost. Now he must step off that throne and kneel before the one who truly occupies it. That is why it is the "humble" whom God beautifies with salvation (Ps. 149:4). The proud cannot be saved, because they cannot get off the throne.

And this is also why salvation is by faith. We who cannot save ourselves rely on Him who can.

Living at the foot of the throne

It is not merely that we believe things God has said. It is far more than that. God has become our everything.

> I am the way, the truth, and the life. No one comes
> to the Father except through Me (John 14:6).

But of Him you are in Christ Jesus, who became

for us wisdom from God—and righteousness and sanctification and redemption (1 Cor. 1:30).

Do you not know that your body is the temple of the Holy Spirit who is in you, whom you have from God, and you are not your own? For you were bought at a price; therefore glorify God in your body and in your spirit, which are God's (1 Cor. 6:19–20).

When Christ who is our life appears, then you also will appear with Him in glory (Col. 3:4).

It is not just that we live with Him—He is our life. It is not just that we live for Him—He lives through us:

I have been crucified with Christ; it is no longer I who live, but Christ lives in me; and the life which I now live in the flesh I live by faith in the Son of God, who loved me and gave Himself for me (Gal 2:20).

Yes, God seats us on the throne again, in Christ. And in Christ, it is our rightful place. But this cannot happen until we have first taken the lowest place.

The loveliness of lowliness

Someone once put it this way: "Despair is the basis of faith." Only when I truly despair of myself, will I truly trust my Savior. I have only so much faith. If some of it is in me, then it isn't all in Him. I remember a song we used to sing when I was a young Christian. "If I tried to live for You, Lord, today" the song began; "If I tried to follow Your wonderful way." The next line always surprised me. Instead of saying: "That would be a very good thing," it said: "Then all of my life would be me, and not You."

Every time we sang the song, I felt I was on the brink of understanding something very deep.

Another time I recall hearing a sermon on the True Vine, from John 15. The preacher explained that the life of the branches (us) came from the sap (the Spirit) in the Vine (Christ). I can still see him staggering around the front of the church, giving an imitation of his first childhood steps.

"This," he said, "is what I'm like when it's me who's doing the walking." We had to let Christ "walk" in us, to live through us. I emerged from the church sure that I had grasped a vital lesson of the Christian walk. But I hadn't—or, at least only very partially. That was a quarter of a century ago. Things seem clearer now, and they're getting clearer all the time.

The apostle says: "I know that in me (that is, in my flesh) nothing good dwells" (Rom. 7:18). I always felt that a harsh statement. *"Nothing good"?* I was sure that I was better than that. Many failures, sins, broken resolutions, and disappointments have taught me to agree with him. Whatever is good is from God, and He gives us so much without our being aware of where it comes from. But what if He should do what He did with Hezekiah—He "withdrew from him, in order to test him, that He might know all that was in his heart"? (2 Chron. 32:31)

As times goes on, God does this to show us what we are in ourselves. I have learned that I can't trust me; I have to trust Christ.

This is the fundamental truth of humility. It comes out of a broken spirit which, like a broken flower, gives off the most beautiful perfume.

Mixing with the great

When I was a ministerial student, I had the marvelous opportunity to spend a month in a famous church. The minister of that church was David Watson, now in heaven. Much of what I did in that month was routine, but there were precious moments spent with David and his fellow-leaders.

On one occasion, I was allowed to be present at a leaders' meeting. David led it, newly returned from speaking at a Bible convention. He had been trying to address divisions among Christians, and had faced sharp opposition.

He sat there pale with fatigue. The leaders surrounded him, gifted and weighty men. All in all, they were a mighty gathering. I listened with rapt attention to every word. When the meeting ended, I served the coffee. Rather than wash the dirty cups as they mounted up, I decided to do that later, and spend every moment I could talking to these great men.

I have emphasized that these were mighty men of God, and not all of them had much time to spend with a mere student. But I did the best I could, and in the end I returned to the sink to wash it all up.

But the sink was already occupied. David Watson stood there, sleeves rolled up, face whiter than ever with exhaustion. He was washing up the dirty cups.

It had seemed natural to him to do the evening's humblest chore. I, who had survived many sermons on humility, was cut to the quick. I realized that I had never taken this "humility stuff" seriously. Was I even taking Christ seriously? I knew now that I *really* wanted to be humble like Jesus.

I can't remember what I learned from talking to those great leaders. But I can still see David Watson washing up as clearly as if it were happening now.

Part company with Samson
Humility is essential. Realistic about our utter bankruptcy, we

trust ourselves fully to God. As a natural consequence, we know all that is good within ourselves to be His gift. We cannot, therefore, be proud of it. How can a beggar be proud of what a good man gives him?

Who knows what temptations we shall face; what tests, what challenges will rock us? If we survive, it will be thanks to Him, the Rock. And we shall survive, because He says He will keep us safe—and for no other reason.

> He only is my rock and my salvation;
> He is my defense;
> I shall not be greatly moved (Ps. 62:2).

It is encouraging to read these words of David. Like Samson, he fell into appalling sin. And yet, at the end, the words of this psalm were fulfilled. David was *not* greatly moved from his security in God. He learned the awful weakness of his flesh (see Ps. 51), but it didn't destroy his confidence—it redirected it. His reliance was entirely on God: "He is my defense."

"If Samson fell, what hope have I?" Might these be your words? We shall see that Samson's fall—hateful though it was— led to great good, both to himself and to Israel. At the end of his life, David recognized that God "makes my way perfect" (2 Sam. 45:33). We too shall say the same. To the true believer, there is this guarantee: "He who has begun a good work in you, will complete it until the day of Jesus Christ" (Phil. 1:6).

FINAL BETRAYAL 10

Judges 16:4-22

Who was Delilah?

It is usually assumed that she was Samson's Philistine woman. Instead, it seems to me that she was his Israelite wife. We haven't much to go on, and whatever our conclusion, we can't be absolutely certain.

Samson's wife . . . or merely his woman?

Some assume that she was a prostitute, but that cannot be the case. "How can you say, 'I love you,'" she demands (Jud. 16:15). Their relationship was not financial—it was one of love, or so Samson assumed. Certainly he "loved" her (v. 4).

But were they man and wife? If so, theirs could hardly have been a normal marriage. Samson could scarcely have advertised that he was married: that would be an invitation to the Philistines to come and take him. After all, marriage was a very public affair, and the Philistines would soon hear about it and know where to find their old enemy. Probably, married or not, he visited Delilah at irregular intervals. No doubt he came after nightfall, after checking around the house for an ambush.

Scripture says that "he loved a woman" (v. 4). If she was his "woman," does that mean she wasn't his wife? Not at all: the word for "woman" here (Hebrew, *ishshah*) is often translated "wife"—in the key texts of Genesis 2:24-25, for instance. You don't even need to say "*his* woman" to convey the sense of "wife."[1] Nothing stops us from translating verse 4 as "he loved [his] wife."

A lot depends on how we view the Samson of the time. He had just been with a prostitute; did he remain at the same low moral level? On the other hand, he was a hero of faith (faith, as we have seen, always leads to good works). Can he have remained impenitent, and have entered two immoral relationships, one after another?

The sin with the prostitute was an isolated fall, like David with Bathsheba. A sudden temptation can overwhelm a normally righteous man. But, were Delilah not Samson's wife, their relationship would have been a continuous sin. Can we really picture this man of faith planning to sin with Delilah, week after week, month after month? Wouldn't his godly conscience have compelled him to halt the relationship?

Delilah the Israelite . . . or the Philistine?

Neither her name nor her living in the Valley of Sorek (v. 4) determine her nationality. Obviously, she was a Philistine in heart, but then what else would one expect from idolatrous Israel at that time? The vital clues come in verse 5. We are told that she was offered 5,500 pieces of silver (1,100 from each of the five Philistine lords)—a vast sum. In Judges 17:10, ten pieces of silver was an attractive annual wage. So 5,500 was more than you could earn in 500 years at that rate. To calculate its modern equivalent, multiply the average wage by 500, and then add 10 percent!

This indicates that Delilah was no Philistine. Samson's Philistine wife would have been expected to betray him without payment—it was her patriotic duty. Actually, she was threatened with burning if she didn't! (Jud. 14:15) As an Israelite, on the other hand, Delilah would have to betray both her husband and her country—hence the enormous bribe.

We are also told in 16:5, that the offer was made by the Philistine lords in person. In ancient times, leaders were very conscious of their dignity. It is unthinkable that they would have come in person, unless every persuasion were needed to win Delilah over. I cannot imagine that they would have dignified a prostitute with such a visit.

All in all, I picture Delilah as an Israelite and Samson's wife.

Why did she betray him?

Although Samson could hardly have lived with Delilah in a normal way, he could have loved her fully. Much of the time Delilah would have lived alone. Samson's visits would have been brief. Even if he were her husband, his visits would have been more like those of a secret lover. But at least he could have loved her.

Verse 4 tells us that he did love her, but he did not appear to give himself entirely to her. I say this because of verse 17, where we hear "that he told her all his heart, and said to her, 'No razor has ever come upon my head, for I have been a Nazirite to God from my mother's womb'" (Jud. 16:17).

Being a Nazirite was no mere detail of Samson's life. It would be impossible to understand him without knowing he was a lifelong Nazirite. Yet here, near the end of their relationship, he tells her "all his heart." Now he informs her of his Nazirite vow.

To some, Delilah's ignorance of Samson's vow proves them to be unmarried. How could they be married, they argue, without her knowing this about her husband? Why had he kept it from her before? Whatever the reason—I'll give my explanation later on—it is clear that she did not have the whole of Samson. She knew he loved her; she used his love to manipulate him (v. 15). But she must have sensed that a part of him was always held back from her.

I suspect too that she used something else to justify her wicked deed. In Gaza the Philistines were out to kill Samson (Jud. 16:2). But the agreement the five lords made with Delilah was that they would only "bind him to afflict him" (v. 5). It may be that she excused herself with that. "I'm saving his life," she may have told herself. "He's bound to get himself killed sooner or later; at least now they'll keep him alive."

This doesn't excuse her betrayal. But perhaps it makes it easier to understand. In any case, Delilah has my pity. We are not told what happened to her, but I cannot imagine anything but sorrow and regret. She would have been a very rich woman, and could have lived anywhere. Anywhere, that is, except Israel, where she would be hated for her betrayal of Samson. Philistine territory wouldn't be safe either. As we shall see, Israel was soon to be on the attack. Delilah would have had to move where Hebrew was not spoken. She would be a foreigner, having to master a new language.

The ancient world did not provide the anonymity of the modern city, so Delilah would be pursued by the tale of her ill deed. On top of all that, God would not hold her innocent for her act. She would face the terrors of a bad conscience and divine punishments—in this world and the next.

In return for all this misery, Delilah had nothing except the money. And had she imagined that money brings happiness, experience would soon disabuse her of the notion.

Yes, we should pity Delilah.

Samson incognito

We may picture Samson in a simple disguise slipping through the trees towards his wife's house. Once inside, he removes his disguise, but only outwardly. The true Samson is still disguised. Delilah doesn't know that he is a lifelong Nazirite. Why did Samson conceal this fact? It must have taken some effort, because local people (whether Israelite or Philistine) would have at least some idea of the Nazirite vow. Samson's long hair, and his refusal of grapes and wine, would be bound to strike some chord of memory.

If the last chapter saw Samson discouraged, he is now more so. Gaza had been a triumph for his strength, but a disaster for his morals. Israel had taken no advantage of Gaza's vulnerability; by now the gates had no doubt been repaired.

I suspect that Samson is thoroughly disillusioned by his life. "What's the point of it all?" he thinks. "Where is it all leading?"

He had not broken his vow, but it was good to forget it, and try to be a bit more normal. The Nazirite vow was just not the sort of thing he wanted to talk about. If Delilah asked about his hair, it was easier to avoid the question than answer it. "Some wine? No thanks, I just don't like it." But the time came when Delilah had to know the truth.

The trap

The plan was this: Delilah would draw forth Samson's secret when he visited her for a night. Then she would use the knowledge to take away his strength. Meanwhile, Philistine soldiers would be waiting in the house, but out of sight. They had to be in the house, because Samson would presumably check for them outside the house as a normal precaution.

As soon as Delilah had rendered Samson strengthless, she would call the soldiers, and he would be taken. Everything depended on learning Samson's secret. Everyone assumed that the answer would be magical: some spell or esoteric action would hold the key.

To start with, Samson resisted. He had no idea that Philistine soldiers were hiding close by, but he knew better than to entrust himself wholly to Delilah. His initial answers were just what Delilah would have expected: "magic" answers.

Magic is the Devil's confidence trick. He has projected a world in which warring spirits control human life. Because these spirits are supposedly disunited, they can be played, one against another, and made to obey certain laws. Man manipulates these spirits—or thinks he does—by using various "magic" items, powerless in themselves. Shapes drawn on the floor and other harmless items are apparently able to control the spirits. Magicians are convinced they are gaining benefit at the expense of these spirits. In reality, they are selling their souls at a cheap price. . . .

Samson told Delilah what she expected to hear. Fresh bowstrings—to the magic number of seven—would undo his power. Such innocent objects as unused ropes, or a loom, could make him powerless. Once Samson was asleep, Delilah attempted each of these "magic spells," and then roused him with a cry of warning. Each time, he broke the securing bonds easily, and the Philistine soldiers remained in hiding. He had no idea that the enemy was so close.

I wonder how the conversation went each time. Perhaps something like this:

Samson: Why did you tie me up?

Delilah: I wanted to see if you were telling me the truth. And you weren't! Why do you lie to me? Why can't you trust me?

Samson: But I do trust you! It's just that, well, some things are best kept secret.

Delilah: You say you love me, but you're just using me. You turn up when you want me, but I'm never allowed really to know you! You're supposed to be my husband, but I don't even know where your strength comes from!

And so it would go. "She pestered him daily with her words and pressed him, so that his soul was vexed to death" (Jud. 16:16). Eventually, Samson told her the truth.

Fortunately, she didn't understand it.

Where was Samson's strength?

He told her all his heart, and said to her, "No razor has ever come upon my head, for I have been a Nazirite to God from my mother's womb. If I am shaven, then my strength will leave me, and I shall become weak, and be like any other man" (Jud. 16:17).

The truth was that Samson's strength came from God. Samson understood that he must trust God, and obey Him, if he wanted God's strength to remain. The Nazirite's hair represented his obedience (cf. Num. 6:18). To shave it was to disobey God.

It seems that Delilah and the Philistines took Samson's words the wrong way. They thought that his long hair was magical in itself and that to remove it would make him powerless. Events seemed to prove them right, but they were in fact wrong.

The point was not how long Samson's hair was, but whether Samson was keeping his holy vow. The issue wasn't hair length, but holiness. Unfortunately for the Philistines, Samson's words were ambiguous. "If I am shaven," he said. Does that mean "If anyone shaves me," or "If I shave myself"? It seems to mean the first. However, in the only other place where this Hebrew form occurs, Jeremiah 41:5, the meaning is clearly "shaving oneself."

The Philistines could keep Samson's hair from ever getting long again. They could shave him whenever they wished. But such forcible shavings did not break the Nazirite vow. Only shaving himself could render Samson unholy.

"But," you will say, "he did not shave himself. Delilah did it." Alas, that is not the whole truth. Whatever Samson said, Delilah did. When Samson linked his hair to his strength, it was clear that Delilah would shave him. It was as if Samson had cut his own hair; broken his own vow.

His head lies fitfully on her lap. Gently she strokes his hair. Quietly she murmurs words of love. Once she is sure that he is asleep, she will call for the man who will shave his head.

At this moment, his breathing is deep and regular. Surely he is asleep. Delilah opens her mouth to call the man. Then his breathing breaks; his head turns upon her lap. He whispers words she cannot grasp. Only the words "love" and "Delilah" sound clear to her.

Once again, her hand smoothes his brow. His breathing returns to its sleep-like depth. His brow smooths; the lines of worry disappear. Delilah decides to wait another few minutes until she is sure that he is deeply asleep. Suddenly, unbidden, the thought comes to her that she could wake him and tell him everything. She is sure that he will be able to deal with the soldiers; she thinks that he will forgive her. For a moment, 5,500 pieces of silver seem nothing next to love. But only for a moment.

"With all that money," thinks Delilah, "I shall be happy." Even as her mind frames the words, she knows it isn't so. But her mind is already made up—there is nothing left but to carry through with the plan.

By now he is fast asleep. It is safe to raise her voice to call the man who is waiting.

Before she does so, she turns her eyes towards her love, giving him one last, long look. For better or worse, this is the man whom she has loved, who loves her. When next she sees him, he will be without his hair, without his eyes.

As for him—he will never see her again.

From Samson's viewpoint, his fall came about because of his infidelity. By telling Delilah about his hair, he had caused his hair to be cut off. He had broken his Nazirite vow.

Delilah's cry roused him from sleep, and he saw the Philistine soldiers all around him. Deep in his heart he must have felt that everything would be different now—now that he had betrayed his vow. But he lunged toward them, full of his usual confidence. To his horror, his amazement, "the Lord had departed from him" (Jud. 16:20). He was no stronger than an ordinary man, and was easily captured. After that came the blinding.

Once that awful thing was done, we should picture Samson in a dark pit of despair.

Why had the hero fallen? Why had God permitted it? Had he failed his life's calling? Was this the end? Samson was brought back to Gaza, walking through the newly restored gates. Blinded, he saw nothing, only heard the scorn and contempt.

"Oh what a fool! What a stupid, mindless fool! Why did You choose me, Lord? And what happens now, now that I've destroyed it all?"

Why?

In his despair, Samson was now drawing close to the secret of strength. In the last chapter, we saw how great gifts can lead to great pride. We saw how hard it must have been for Samson to keep himself lowly and humble.

Sadly, we humans are all too prone to pride. Unless that pride were dealt with, Samson could never have fulfilled his calling. Now, in the midst of his anguish and defeat, he was being led into something new and utterly beautiful. God was reversing the pride of the fall; God was preparing Samson for his greatest feat.

In the last great blaze of his glory, Samson would show a truly heavenly splendor.

Humbling the great

We are all great, because we are children of the living God. But we have much to learn from those such as Samson. The Apostle Paul is another great man. How could God have called Paul to be His apostle? He had persecuted the church. He had not spent the years with Jesus that others had. Actually, God used Paul more than any of the other apostles (1 Cor. 15:10; 2 Peter 3:15). He was given remarkable insights. Wonderful as these were for us, who benefit so much from them, they presented a problem to Paul.

How could he remain humble before God? God is not one to abandon us to the ravages of pride; He came to Paul's aid.

In 2 Corinthians 12:1-4, Paul speaks of his marvelous revelations. Then he tells us that God acted, "lest I should be exalted above measure by the abundance of the revelations" (v. 7). What did God do to rescue His beloved friend? "A thorn in the flesh was given to me, a messenger of Satan to buffet me, lest I be exalted above measure."

Some may ask whether this "thorn" (literally a "stake"), this messenger (literally "angel") of Satan, was really a gift from God. Who needs that kind of anguish? What good can a messenger of Satan do us? The answer is that Paul was humbled. Without humility, none of us can enjoy friendship with God. Whatever leads to humility is our friend.

What was the thorn?

The thorn was in the apostle's "flesh." The "flesh," in Paul's writings, is either his body, or his "old nature." This gives us two possibilities: the thorn may have been an ailment in Paul's physical body. He could have had a chronic sickness that remained unhealed. The other possibility is that he had a weakness in his old nature. Such a weakness is described in Romans 7:14-24. There, Paul says: "I am carnal" (i.e., "fleshly").

What would this mean? Paul would have been rocked by powerful temptations, his "flesh" siding with them against God. Instead of casting off the temptations with a confident "Get behind me, Satan," he would have faced a terrible inner turmoil.

Imagine that Paul's main temptation was to anger. This thorn would mean that the temptation came with enormous power. Paul need not have actually lost his temper to have felt miserable. He might sometimes have entertained the anger within, with nothing showing externally. He might have felt that he would have lost his temper but for some providential event. He might have had to pray at great length each time, feeling his flesh strongly siding with the anger.

In other words, I am not suggesting that Paul actually

sinned a lot. That wouldn't fit with what he says elsewhere of Christ's power to keep us (see Rom. 6). Perhaps his experience was like that of the apostles in the storm. Their boat filled with water, and seemed about to sink. They had all the misery of a shipwreck without actually having one—because Christ stilled the storm with a word. But it had nevertheless been a dreadful experience. The apostles learned that you don't always feel very safe in a boat, but Jesus always protects you.

Perhaps Paul's thorn taught him just that about his own flesh. You can never feel secure (from temptation) while in this flesh, but the Spirit is always with us to protect us! "The flesh lusts against the Spirit," says Paul, "and the Spirit against the flesh; and these are contrary to one another, so that you do not do the things that you wish" (Gal. 5:17). Only if we "walk in the Spirit" shall we "not fulfill the lust of the flesh" (v. 16). The old masters of the Word called this an "irreconcilable war," in which "the remaining corruption, for a time, may much prevail."[2]

To a godly man, it is sheer misery when "what I will to do, that I do not practice; but what I hate, that I do" (Rom. 7:15). Such an experience would leave Paul desperately weak, utterly cast upon God, entirely reliant upon Him. He would have been forced to turn to God, and plead for deliverance. "O wretched man that I am!" he would have cried. "Who will deliver me from this body of death?" (Rom. 7:24)

So, was it sickness or temptation? It is impossible to say for certain. I think that the Holy Spirit has left the matter unclear so that all of us can identify with Paul.

It is clear how the passage applies to Samson. He was humbled by the weakness of his flesh—the sinfulness of his old nature. His eyes—now gone forever—had led him to the wrong people.

Why had he loved the Philistine woman of Timnah? He might otherwise have married a godly Israelite woman and been spared so much loneliness and anguish.

Why had he gazed at that prostitute in Gaza? His sin with her had weakened him.

Why had he loved Delilah? She had coaxed his secret from him. By loving her he had betrayed God—the only One who truly loved him.

What do you do with a thorn?

Paul tells us that he prayed for the thorn to be taken away (2 Cor. 12:8). Of course he did. Whatever it was, it must have been a dreadfully painful experience. God's answer, however, was "No." This feels very strange to us: whether strong temptation, or chronic sickness, this thorn was a "messenger of Satan"—surely God would remove it!

Why didn't He? The "thorn" left Paul weak, and that was just what he needed. God told him: "My grace is sufficient for you, for My strength is made perfect in weakness" (v. 9). The weaker Paul felt, the more he had to rely on his Lord.

Now we must admit that our natural reaction is to be rid of our weaknesses if we can. At least we would rather not dwell upon them. In fact, the climate of our age is against being weak. Christian leaders feel the pressure to appear beyond such weaknesses. If we hear a great leader speak, we just can't imagine them oversleeping and missing their time of prayer. How could they ever be weak, discouraged, fleshly? Surely they would never be moody and distant over the breakfast table! They could never feel far from God; they could never feel overwhelmed by temptations!

They say no such thing, but we assume it. We are living in an age when we are not impressed with weakness.

This has not always been the case. The great Christian heroes of the past have been more than willing to speak of their weakness. Some of the greatest leaders the church has ever had have been full of a sense of their own unworthiness.

John Chrysostom (fourth century) was the obvious choice to lead the church in Constantinople. But he knew better—or, rather, worse—about himself. He fled the city in order to avoid a spiritual dignity too high for him. In spite of that, he did lead the Constantinople church. His wonderful biblical teaching earned him the name Chrysostom—"golden-tongued"—and has been read avidly ever since.

His classic book *On the Priesthood* describes the work of the ministry. It also explains why he tried to avoid church leadership. The simple fact is, he felt he wasn't worthy of such a high calling. An enduring sense of his own unworthiness made him a wonderful leader.

Bernard of Clairvaux (twelfth century) was a truly remarkable man. He combined strengths that few men have had. As a theologian, he was outstanding. The sixteenth-century reformers, such as Luther and Calvin, singled him out from his medieval contemporaries as a great Bible teacher. He was persuaded to face Abelard (a forerunner of today's liberal theologians) in a theological debate, and won an unexpected victory.

As a popular preacher, Bernard set his generation alight. But he was also a great miracle worker. Over fifty striking miracles were performed by him on one day and recorded by eyewitnesses. These included raising the dead.

As well as all this, no one had the international influence Bernard had. He could mediate between armies, and avert wars. Kings listened to him with respect, because they knew that God listened to his prayers.

So, what sort of man was Bernard? His writings reveal a man who is desperately weak. His motto was: "Love to be unknown," and unknown he would have remained, had God not thrust him into the public eye. He was so appalled by his own weaknesses that he just wanted to be alone with God and be healed.

His classic book, *Twelve Steps of Humility and Pride*,[3] makes the point. He begins by describing the subtleties of human pride, as one who knows it all too well. When the time comes to describe humility, he excuses himself and draws the book to a close instead.

The modern reader stands perplexed. Anyone who can expose the intricacies of pride must be an expert on humility. Why won't Bernard talk about it? "I can but teach what I have learned," he says (p. 70). "I am aware that my own movements tend to be down rather than up." If his readers would learn about humility, he refers them to another writer.

When I first read these words, I was stunned. Obviously Bernard knew more about humility than I could ever imagine knowing. But he says he knows nothing. What then do I know? I felt astonished and frightened. Reading about pride had been a nasty shock. Much in me that I had wished to remain covered had been unearthed. I was prepared to admit that I wasn't very humble. Now it appeared that I knew much less than a man who knew "nothing."

Bernard had learned a rare lesson in Christlike humility. Few Christians have confronted their world with Jesus as he did. We have so much to learn from him.

Don't hate the thorn

Paul had wished his thorn gone. Then he learned that it would help him to be humble, "lest I be exalted above measure." So what was his new attitude to this "messenger of Satan"? "Most gladly," he says, "I will rather boast in my infirmities" (v. 9); "I take pleasure in infirmities" (v. 10).

This is not what we expect to hear. How does a great Christian leader face an attack from a "messenger of Satan"? Surely we shall hear about some glorious victory, with the "messenger" retreating in confusion. There must be some method of prayer, some special faith, that wins the victory.

Instead, the messenger of Satan remains. Paul is weakened as a result. But it is just Paul who is weakened, not God. God's "strength is made perfect in weakness" (v. 9). The weaker Paul becomes (in his own eyes), the more he must rely on his Savior. "When I am weak, then I am strong," he says (v. 10). Why? Because his desperate weakness forces him upon his God.

Something similar was happening with Samson. "Out of weakness," the Holy Spirit says, they "were made strong" (Heb. 11:34). Now he knew failure. His mouth was filled with the bitter taste of defeat. His own sinful foolishness had been his downfall. He had lost sight and strength. He was finished, that much was clear.

Or was it? Might God still have a purpose for Samson? God had said that Samson would begin to deliver Israel from the Philistines. Could it be that God would have His own way, in spite of Samson's total weakness? Is God strong enough to use a feeble blind man? If He did, the glory would be God's alone, not the blind man's.

Our section of Judges ends with Samson a wretched prisoner. He is chained and consigned to hard labor. He is surely a broken man. The Philistines, who have suffered so much from him over the years, will hope to use him now to raise their national morale.

The Philistines had thought Samson's hair magical. They would never allow him to grow it long again. Perhaps they cut it regularly, who knows? Would it have made a difference? The point is, as Scripture tells us, "The hair of his head began to grow again after it had been shaven" (Jud. 16:22).

Blind and broken, Samson has restarted his Nazirite vow. He will not cut his hair, nor do anything to encourage anyone else to cut it. Will he succeed now, where he failed before? He now has two great advantages: he cannot *see* to desire the wrong women, and he has tasted utter defeat. This shattered figure in chains is more of a threat than ever before.

Being brought low

I don't think any of us find it easy when we are brought low. We want to imitate Jesus in His miracles and His success. We don't want to follow Him who "learned obedience by the things which He suffered" (Heb. 5:8). Powerful Jesus, who fed the crowds and healed the sick, is a wonderful example. Desolate Jesus, hanging alone on the cross, crying in anguish, is another matter.

> It is good for a man to bear the yoke in his youth.
> Let him sit alone and keep silent,
> Because God has laid it on him;
> Let him put his mouth in the dust—
> There may yet be hope (Lam. 3:27-29).

Does it seem "good" to you? Wouldn't you rather go on to the victory and the glory? Samson went straight to power and success, without his "mouth in the dust" in failure. But, without that "yoke in his youth," he had to bear it at the end of his life. "There may yet be hope," Jeremiah says. Indeed there may be— there was for Samson and Paul, and there will be for us.

Don't refuse the suffering. Don't despair when God allows you to see how utterly empty we all are apart from Him. Don't sink into sadness—it is God's way with those He loves. It seems to be the only way to free us from the godlike assumptions we have inherited from old father Adam.

> For His anger is but for a moment,
> His favor is for life;
> Weeping may endure for a night,
> But joy comes in the morning (Ps. 30:5).

Yes, there is a glorious sunrise for us. First we see ourselves and weep in the ghastly gloom of night, but then comes the joy!

---

1. In Judges, for instance, the wives of Achsah (1:12-13), Lapidoth (4:4), Heber (4:17) and Gilead (11:2) are simply called "woman" (or "wife," Hebrew, "*ishshah*").
2. The 1646 Westminster Confession of Faith, chapter 13, section 3.
3. Translated by H.C. Backhouse (Hodder and Stoughten, 1985).

SUNDOWN

Judges 16:23-30

How can you blame me? I am only a youngster. I am no officer, no leader. I am no priest, no wise man. How was I supposed to know?

They told me to hold the slave's hand and guide him. When they took me to his cell, I was terrified, I can tell you. But when I saw him, it wasn't so bad. Of course, he was blind. Instead of those terrifying eyes people talk about, there were just empty sockets.

He didn't know who had been led into his cell. He just sat patiently, his face serene. I somehow thought we'd interrupted him praying to his God.

They told me not to worry about him. Without his long magic hair, he was supposed to be no stronger than anyone else. "He's no danger now"—those were the very words they used.

How was I supposed to know? Am I a prophet like that Israelite Samuel?

Anyway, he didn't look dangerous. When they said he had to perform at the feast, he didn't argue. I took his hand and led him out, meek as a lamb.

How everyone laughed at him! I thought he would get

angry then, but he didn't. It looked as if something had died within him; he just seemed a defeated man.

Well, after a while, when the slave wouldn't get angry, they got bored. They told him he could stop, and I led him aside. When he spoke to me, I was amazed at how gentle his voice was. "Let me feel the pillars which support the temple," he said, "so that I can lean on them."

So now you're telling me I should have read his mind? He fooled our leaders—how was I supposed to see through him? I guess we all thought he'd lost his brains when he lost his strength.

But he never gave the slightest clue! He just seemed tired. The way he said it, I thought he wanted to feel the grandeur of our glorious temple. He'd never been inside before, although I had heard him asking for the details of its structure.

How was I supposed to know that the building depended on those pillars? I'm not a builder! These things are too much for me to understand.

He should have been exhausted after all they'd made him do. He leaned against the pillars, as if he needed support. His hands felt the stone. I told him how glorious the temple was, but he seemed to be concentrating on something else.

When his voice thundered forth, I thought my heart would stop. I'd never heard anything like it before. Everyone was quiet for an instant, as he called on his God.

Then came the laughter. I thought the slave was going to burst with frustration, but then I realized that his chest was heaving with effort: he was between the pillars, trying to push them apart. Of course, even with his magic strength he couldn't have budged them an inch.

People laughed even more. Without his magic, the slave was pathetic. But the laughter ceased at the first *crack*.

That awful moment! It's something I'll never forget as long

as I live. The *crack* came from the roof, and it was as sharp as a charioteer's whip.

Suddenly all eyes were on the slave. His mighty arms were at full stretch now, and the immovable weight of the pillars submitted to his relentless will. I have never seen such an effort! His muscles stood out like dragons' tendons. Even were a god to come to earth, I don't believe you'd see such power!

Strangely enough, utter repose covered his face. He looked the same as he had praying in his cell—except, there was something new in his expression. It was joy, joy like a mighty torrent.

I remember thinking: "This man is going to die. How can he be joyful?"

Suddenly the officers roused themselves. Orders were shouted, and soldiers leapt forward to grab the slave.

Too late, far too late by now.

The pillars were falling, and with them the whole roof. The noise was indescribable. Everyone was screaming and trying to get to safety.

No one but me survived, and I think myself blessed by the gods that I was not worse hurt.

The last thing I saw before I became unconscious was the slave. He had not moved from his spot between the pillars. His great head was lifted up and his sightless face gazed aloft.

I heard him give a great cry of joy, as if he were welcoming his God, and then he died.

I swear I have never seen such peace and joy—yes, and gratitude—on a human face.

With the fall of Dagon's temple, the officers and leaders of the Philistines were destroyed (Jud. 16:27, 30) Three thousand perished. Philistia became like a body without a head. Samson had fulfilled his calling; he had begun to deliver Israel out of the hand of the Philistines.

What changed this strengthless slave into such a savage scourge? It was this: Samson prayed (Judg. 16:28). That prayer destroyed the head of Israel's enemies. It would be well to examine it in detail.

"O Lord God, remember me, I pray!"

Not so long ago, Samson had presumed on God's presence, but found that "the Lord had departed from him" (Jud. 16:20). His pride had assumed that God would help—even though Samson had betrayed his Nazirite vow. Now he presumed nothing. He began by begging God to hold him in his thoughts.

"I am poor and needy," says David, "yet the Lord thinks upon me" (Ps. 40:17). Why should God think upon such a wretched figure as Samson? How could Samson have dared to ask that He should?

It couldn't be because of his faithfulness, because he had been unfaithful. It couldn't be his heroic victories, because now he had brought shameful defeat upon himself. It couldn't be his righteousness: he had been with a prostitute, and then broken his Nazirite vow.

So, why should God hold Samson in His loving thoughts?

I suspect that Samson, in his defeat, had learned what we must all learn: that God's love is unconditional. This is a lesson that is hard to master. God will teach us, but only when we are in the lowest place.

How can I believe that God loves me for no reason except that He loves me? "The Lord did not set His love on you nor choose you," the Spirit tells Israel, "because you were more in number than any other people, for you were the least of all peoples" (Deut. 7:7). Well, why did He love them? Here is the reason: "But because the Lord loves you" (v. 8).

He loves us because He loves us.

My successes earn me nothing—how could they? Everything good in me is God's gift. "You have also done all our works in us" (Isa. 26:12). Not just our actions, but our very desire to do good is God's gift: "It is God who works in you both to will and to do for His good pleasure" (Phil. 2:13).

My sins and failures do not quench God's love. Jesus is "the Lamb slain from the foundation of the world" (Rev. 13:8). He died for our sins 2,000 years ago, so why say He was "slain from the foundation of the world"? It is to emphasize that His death was no last-minute impulse. He knew we would sin. He loved us anyway. So He planned to die from the very beginning.

"O Lord God, remember me, I pray!" cried Samson. Remember me, because You are "merciful and gracious, long-suffering, and abounding in goodness and truth" (Ex. 34:6). I am broken and lost; I've seen at last the depths of my human sinfulness. I have nothing to be proud of; I've earned nothing. But remember me, because You are so good and kind. You love me because You love me.

"Strengthen me, I pray, just this once, O God"

Samson had his supernatural strength for so long that it must have seemed part of him. When he sinned it away, he realized that it had been a gift all along. It is all too easy for us to forget where all good things come from.

From the beginning of my Christian life, I understood that God wanted me to seek Him daily. I also found that I had to get up early to pray and study the Scriptures—otherwise I never got around to it. For many years I battled, fairly unsuccessfully, with my innate laziness. When God stepped in and changed all that, it seemed like a gift descending directly from heaven. I was the astonished spectator, watching myself rising early, day after day!

After a while, this became part of ordinary life. Sadly, I

began to think that this was now "part of me," an inherent strength. This meant that I could now act in a superior way toward others in the ministry who lacked this discipline. "Get a little discipline," I would say from my position of lofty eminence.

It must have seemed to God that I was now so strong in myself that I hardly needed His help. The special gift disappeared. Now I found that I didn't get up to seek God. I found, as Hezekiah had done, that "God withdrew from him, in order to test him, that he might know all that was in his heart" (2 Chron. 32:31).

After a while this new state became really intolerable. It had gone on too long to be merely a "tired phase." I could remember getting up daily and really enjoying God's beautiful presence. I just couldn't do it now. Half the time I didn't really want to. I was shocked and grieved at my hard heart. I tried "pulling myself together," and indeed all the things I had told others, but nothing worked.

I found myself praying Isaiah's prayer:

> O Lord, why have You made us stray from Your ways,
> And hardened our heart from Your fear? (Isa. 63:17)

I now realized that this grace of discipline had been God's gift all the time—not an inherent strength in me. He had given an eager heart to seek Him—and then withdrawn it. Of course, I had nothing to blame God for. My hard heart is my fault. But by withdrawing His special help, He had let me stray from His ways.

Samson's prayer became mine: "Strengthen me, I pray!" In due course, God answered it. By then, I had learned where such good gifts come from. "And what do you have that you did not receive? Now if you did indeed receive it, why do you boast as if you had not received it?" (1 Cor. 4:7)

Perhaps this is why Samson added "just this once." Of course, he expected to die, so he would only need strength one more time. But perhaps too he understood that his strength had always been a moment-by-moment gift. Each time God had given it "just this once."

"That I may with one blow take vengeance"

Samson's motive may seem to be mere vengeance. Stephen died with a prayer of forgiveness on his lips—surely this is better than Samson's vengefulness. We should not forget, however, that he was a judge. The Bible adds, a couple of verses later, "He had judged Israel twenty years" (Jud. 16:31).

Remember that a judge had to execute God's just laws. By blinding Samson, the Philistines had rendered Israel leaderless. Samson had always been Israel's leader in battle, even though none had followed him. On the judicial principle of "an eye for an eye," Samson—God's appointed judge—must render Philistia leaderless.

We, of course, must act like Stephen because, as private citizens, we cannot take the law into our own hands. So what can we learn from Samson's prayer?

First, we can learn to pray for just and righteous law in our land. Western Europe was once governed by unjust pagan law, but Christian revivals through the Middle Ages changed all that. Although Western European law was never entirely biblical, it was far more wholesome than it is now. If God did that once, He can do it again. Let us pray that He will, and be prepared to play our part.

Second, remember that God's Law is His will. Samson was

praying that God would have His own way. It was more than mere personal vengeance. Samson the judge always sought God's justice. "It is written, 'Vengeance is mine, I will repay,' says the Lord" (Rom. 12:19).

In other words, Samson was echoing Jesus' prayer: "Your will be done" (Matt. 6:10; 26:42). Samson knew what was going to happen to him. "Let me die with the Philistines!" he cried (Jud. 16:30).

Although Samson had never been in Dagon's temple, he had apparently mastered its architectural structure from the descriptions of others. He realized that he had a chance to fulfill his calling if God were to restore his strength. But what would happen to him?

It would have been far more pleasant to have survived. Surely, with the leadership of the Philistines gone, Israel would be bound to throw off its servitude. Samson would be greeted by a grateful, appreciative people. At last he would gain the applause that had ever been denied him. His blindness meant that his labors were over. He could retire, waited on by a thankful Israel.

Although blind, he would hear the heroics of Samson—the "sunlike"—celebrated in the people's songs. His would be a gracious sunset for a living legend.

Did such thoughts come into his mind as he framed his prayer? Did he nearly pray: "Destroy the Philistines, Lord, but let me live"? Once before (Jud. 15:18) he had prayed for a miraculous deliverance, and his life had been saved. It wasn't wrong then; would it be so wrong now?

When Samson cried "Let me die!" He joined a select group of heroes. Jesus is the supreme hero: He died for our sins. But there have been others who died for God's people. At this moment, Samson joins that group.

When the Apostle Paul thought about such matters, he felt "a desire to depart and be with Christ, which is far better" (Phil. 1:23). But he concluded that "to remain in the flesh is more needful for you" (v. 24). For Samson, it was otherwise. He knew that his death would galvanize Israel into action, which was far better than his continuing life as a blind man. The heroic death of a leader always puts fresh courage into his followers. So Samson could serve his Lord best by dying.

Already on the threshold of glory, Samson sees his way clear at last. He sees his death, but its dark and painful tones are dim next to the glory set before him. Beyond his death, he sees Israel roused from servile cowardice. He sees his name on the lips of thousands of fierce warriors.

But now, such earthly matters have lost their prominence. As never before, he sees the God who is the center of all things. It is not hard to let go his grip on worldly things. Israel's well-being is in God's hand. However mysterious the divine plan seems, Samson now feels no doubt that it shall be fulfilled.

In fact, the plan has been fulfilled in Samson's life. He sees his own weakness in a new light. God's plan allowed for it—even used it. Indeed his betrayal of the Nazirite vow fit into the plan. How else could he have been permitted to stand by the pillars of the temple, with all of the Philistine leadership at his mercy?

But already such earthly concerns are fading from Samson's view. The idolatrous temple and its pagan worshipers are like a thin curtain which is already being drawn aside. He is on the threshold of the true temple. Even as his muscles flex with supernatural strength, his sightless eyes gaze beyond all temporal things.

He sees things none of us has yet seen. Perhaps, like Stephen, he sees "the heavens opened and the Son of Man standing at the right hand of God!" (Acts 7:56) Even as he gives his life for God's people, he sees the One whom he is imitating. The Son of Man, slain from before the foundation of the world, stands to welcome him. Samson knows where he got the willingness to die, as he looks into his Savior's eyes.

But his story is now passing beyond the confines of this world and our vision. Even as the temple's demolition thunders doom for the Philistines, so I imagine a thunderous welcome in our eternal home, as this great hero finishes his course.

Dying to live

What have we learned of the secret of strength? We have seen Samson receiving supernatural strength early in his life. We have seen him learn the dreadful lesson of the weakness of the flesh. We have seen him complete his education in the dungeons of the Philistines.

We have heard his last grand prayer and watched him demolish God's enemies. The secret is now fully his—but his life is over. Surely, the secret of strength will mark the beginning of life in its fullness—not its end! Surely, when we are truly strong, we can truly live.

As a young Christian, I imagined God giving me great gifts and strengths. I pictured myself doing grand exploits—for Him, of course! My self interest in such things is very clear to me now. What I didn't realize is that it isn't merely a matter of God giving us things. God gives us Himself.

As He draws closer to us, so we become closer to Him. The more we are one with Him, the more we submit to His will. It is His name which we hold holy; His kingly rule which we want; His will which we desire.

> I have been crucified with Christ;
> it is no longer I who live, but Christ lives in me;

and the life which I now live in the flesh
I live by faith in the Son of God,
who loved me and gave Himself for me
(Gal. 2:20).

It is not that we "merge with the infinite" in a Buddhist or New Age sense. We will always be ourselves, emphatically distinct from everyone else. But our desire becomes more and more for God to have His way. We have grown to love Him, and utterly to admire Him. By contrast, we grow less and less impressed with ourselves. We know, from bitter experience, what we are like when we have our own way (Rom. 7:14-23).

This is a kind of death: "I have been crucified with Christ." "Whoever loses his life for My sake will find it" (Matt. 16:25). Not death in the sense of ceasing to exist, but death to me running my own life.

If necessary, we will give our lives for Christ's sake. If called we shall do mighty exploits for Jesus; we are equally willing to suffer for Him. "For to you it has been granted on behalf of Christ, not only to believe in Him, but also to suffer for His sake" (Phil. 1:29).

So the ball is in your court. Do you really want the secret of strength? Are you ready to lay down your own desires, plans, and ambitions? If you do, tell your Lord. Read again Samson's last prayer, and tell the Lord that you would wish to "amen" it for yourself. Whatever the sacrifices, you will know a joy known only to the true servants of Jesus.

12 AFTERMATH

Judges 16:31

They came while we were searching through the wreckage. I shall never forget that day. In one awful stroke all our leaders were lost. Nobody knew what to do, so we began to dig among the ruins. We thought we could at least bury our lords with some honor.

The only comfort was that the hero was gone for good.

It was an hour before daybreak and the thunder was growling uneasily, when we saw them coming from the eastern hills. No one wanted to let them through, but no one dared stop them either. You had only to look at them to see they were the hero's kin. Worse still, they had his eyes. I thought I knew one of them, but perhaps I was wrong. He used to walk with eyes downcast, tamely subdued to our rule. If it was the same man, he was much changed.

He strode up to me and fixed me with his eyes. News of the great disaster had sped to their camp, and he demanded to know where the hero lay.

For a moment, I was too terrified to speak or move. I must have stuttered something, because the whole group came over to me, and told me to speak up. None of our own folk dared stand with me.

As I looked from blazing eye to blazing eye, I realized that the hero wasn't gone after all. Their fury seared me to the very soul. I knew then that they had lost their fear of us. I tried to tell them about the pillars, but they didn't hear me out. They turned contemptuously and strode into the ruins. I should have been insulted, but all I can remember feeling is relief.

They found the hero's body surprisingly undamaged. I caught a glimpse of his mighty face. Clearly, he had greeted death without fear. In fact, his last moment had been one of joy—that was clear from his expression.

Our talk was hushed as they raised up his body. In that eerie silence, they wept aloud. Then, moving slowly, they began the long journey home. Still none of us dared speak. As they made their way toward the mountains, one turned back to look at me.

Behind him, the sun was rising, illuminating a clear sky above the mountains. It was as if light were dawning for them, while darkness was reserved for us. He looked at me with the hero's eyes.

I knew he'd be back.

I knew they'd all be back.

Samson's body was laid in his father's tomb. I imagine his family there, and many others too. Many who had lived their lives in cowardice and submission must have wept bitter tears. Someone would have recounted Samson's wonderful deeds. When he came to the last and greatest victory, the shame would have been too great for many there.

They had failed their God, and tamely submitted to the rule of Dagon's people. Samson's life became an eloquent sermon that devastated them.

We pick up the story as it continues in 1 Samuel 7. At that time, "all the house of Israel lamented after the Lord" (v. 2). The shame that Samson's death must have provoked mingled with their other humiliations. The ark was still not returned to the tabernacle. That highlighted their failure: they had failed their God and were in disgrace. They were the servants of invaders, in the land that God had promised to them.

It was time to act.

> Then Samuel spoke to all the house of Israel, saying, "If you return to the Lord with all your hearts, then put away the foreign gods and the Ashtoreths from among you, and prepare your hearts for the Lord, and serve Him only; and He will deliver you from the hand of the Philistines" (1 Sam. 7:3).

This was Samuel's first entrance to the world of politics. The people had learned to trust Samuel. "The Lord was with him and let none of his words fall to the ground. And all Israel from Dan to Beersheba knew that Samuel had been established as a prophet of the Lord" (1 Sam. 3:19-20).

The time was right for the people to respond. They did indeed return to the Lord (1 Sam. 7:4). Samuel organized a special meeting for all the people at Mizpah. There they wept in penitence.

The Philistines, led by newly promoted lords, hastened to attack, and the Israelites were frightened—but not for long. The people stayed with Samuel as he prayed and sacrificed on their behalf. Then the Philistines drew close to God's repentant people. He answered His enemy's threat with terrifying thunder.

The Israelites leaped forth, and won their first victory in

forty years. For some it was the first victory ever.

Samuel had won; Israel had won; Samson had won.

The Philistines were subdued (1 Sam. 7:13-14). Israel faced them again in subsequent eras; they faced other enemies too. It is enough that we win today's battle; our children will have other challenges.

He always leads us in triumph

Here, at the end of the story, we see what was certain from the beginning. God always wins, and we always win in Him. If Samson ever doubted it, he certainly lived to see his mission fulfilled.

"We know that all things work together for good to those who love God, to those who are called according to His purpose" (Rom. 8:28). Yes, we "know" it—even though it doesn't look that way sometimes. Paul, who spoke those words, had known grim opposition, persecution, imprisonment, and the Gospel rejected by many. How can that be good?

In 2 Corinthians 2:14, he says: "Thanks be to God who always leads us in triumph in Christ, and through us diffuses the fragrance of His knowledge in every place." But what about those who reject God? That lovely "fragrance" is an "aroma of death" to them (v. 15), he says. But it is still a victory that they smell it at all.

The point is this: God's plan includes wicked people and wicked deeds. Yes, God has made known His will: everyone ought to keep the Ten Commandments. That is His *revealed* will. But He also has a hidden will: "The secret things belong to the Lord our God, but those things which are revealed belong to us and to our children forever, that we may do all the words of this Law" (Deut. 29:29).

In other words, God has created a world in which there would be much evil. This came as no surprise to Him—it fit into

His plan, hateful though evil is. People do bad things entirely of their own free will. They know nothing of God's plan; if they did, they wouldn't wish to fulfill it. And yet, in spite of their wishes, they do fulfill it. God is so infinitely wise and powerful!

If this is hard to understand, look at Calvary. The courage, love, and compassion of the crucified Christ are the most beautiful sight we can possibly see. But without evil, there could have been no Calvary. Someone had to betray Him, He had to be condemned unjustly, He had to be sentenced to a barbaric death. There had to be hypocritical priests to mock Him.

Now all these evil things were part of the plan—indeed they are predicted in the Scriptures (see Ps. 22 and Acts 1:20, for instance). So far as God's revealed will is concerned, these evil things were hated by God. But in His "secret" will, they were necessary. He planned to permit them, and predicted them in the Old Testament.

Calvary shows us how evil can have its own way, and God still wins. Satan seems to succeed by getting rid of Jesus—only to find Him resurrected and able to save sinners through His death! We see the same in Samson's story. His broken vow, Delilah's betrayal, the cruel blinding and ridicule—all these led to Samson standing by the pillars of the temple with victory in his grasp. Samson's sin and suffering taught him essential lessons about God's grace and our weakness.

So all things did work together for good in Samson's life. And they do in your life too.

Our lives are like beautiful paintings. The brightest colors need dark shades in order that they may appear brighter yet. Our failures and weaknesses, sins and mistakes; these all make God's wonderful grace and salvation appear all the brighter. Just as Samson's life ended in victory, so too will ours. The longer the apparent defeat continues, the greater the eventual victory.

The secret plan in the early church

The early church was born into a Roman Empire which embraced paganism. Philosophy had explored paganism, with all its contradictions and empty promises, and was almost ready to discard it. Instead of welcoming the Gospel, however, it fiercely opposed it. Wickedness triumphed in cruel persecutions.

Naturally the Christians pleaded with God, but He permitted the evil persecutors to continue unchecked. Was this a defeat? In due course, paganism collapsed, and the truth triumphed. But more suffering was still to come. Arianism, a depraved version of Christianity which denied Jesus' divinity, became the new persecutor.

How the believers must have longed for the all-powerful God to put things right!

Several centuries passed before all these enemies were overcome. The truth won in the end, and the church emerged victorious. But why had God permitted so much suffering?

It is easy to see the benefits of this suffering. The earliest centuries of the church were its most vulnerable. Had life been easy for Christians, perhaps the truth would have been mingled with the fashionable paganism of the day. To avert the danger, God kept His church a martyr church for those centuries. The leaders weren't highly paid theologians, keen to introduce their own clever inventions. They were the target of the persecutors; purified by suffering.

Over these centuries, the united martyr church of Jesus Christ laid down standards of Christian doctrine and practice that have helped the church ever since. When Christians say the well-known creeds, they have little idea how much godly suffering, biblical study, and holy living went into them.

Perhaps the greatest of these wonderful leaders was Augustine of Hippo.

Augustine's conversion

Augustine's conversion is one of the great stories of church history. Augustine was born to a pagan father and a Christian mother, Monica. Monica never ceased to pray for her son, and it seemed that as a youngster, he might follow in his mother's faith. Things however went from bad to worse.

Rather than seeking Christ, Augustine adopted a fashionable sub-Christian cult. It was inward looking, super-spiritual, and ideally suited to his intellectual pride. Rather than marry, Augustine lived with his girlfriend. His mother was very sad, but God encouraged her with a vision. In the vision, she saw Augustine following her on a ruler (the mathematical instrument). The ruler was the symbol of the true Christian faith in those days. Monica believed that her son would come to true faith in the true God.

Years passed, with the non-Christian Augustine in his thirties, and his mother neared death. Monica did indeed die, but not before she saw her son converted. Augustine was not easily converted. God even had to send him an audible message, telling him to read the Bible to overcome his unbelief!

When at last he was a believer, Monica's faith had triumphed.

But the triumph was far greater than Monica could possibly have believed. Augustine lived at the great high point of early church theology. His own foolishness and sinful blindness, which had dominated him for so many years, left a lasting impression. Mistrustful of himself, he followed Christ with a lovely humility. That made it possible for God to use his enormous intellect to complete the foundation of early church theology.

He certainly walked on the ruler of true biblical theology! Augustine's books proved so anointed that they underlie all the spiritual advances in the West for at least a thousand years. The spiritual giants of the Middle Ages (Anselm, Bernard, and Aquinas) drew much from his works. The great Reformers of the church (Wycliffe, Huss, Luther, Calvin, and others) acknowledge their debt to him.

Yes, Monica's prayers were answered! The years of "defeat," when Augustine remained unconverted, were really part of the victory. They helped to form a man who knew he had been so wrong for so long; a man who went to God's Word in humility rather than rely on his own ideas.

So how about us? Yes, all things work together for our good too. If we don't see it yet, and usually we don't, let us at least believe it. God is faithful.

The Holy Spirit's last word

It is fitting that some words be said when a great man's body is laid to rest in its grave. The Holy Spirit has not recorded the words men spoke at that time, reserving to Himself the speaking of the last words. He does however say this of Samson and his fellow heroes:

> Who through faith subdued kingdoms, worked righteousness, obtained promises, stopped the mouths of lions, quenched the violence of fire, escaped the edge of the sword, out of weakness were made strong, became valiant in battle, turned to flight the armies of the aliens. Women received their dead raised to life again. Others were tortured, not accepting deliverance, that they might obtain a better resurrection. Still others had trial of mockings and scourgings, yes, and of chains and imprisonment. They were stoned, they were sawed in two, were tempted, were

slain with the sword. They wandered about in
sheepskins and goatskins, being destitute, afflicted,
tormented—of whom the world was not worthy.
They wandered in deserts and mountains, in dens
and caves of the earth (Heb. 11:33-38).

Some of these statements apply directly to Samson, and we
should note them well, keeping the memory of one whom God
has set before us as an example.

Samson did indeed subdue a kingdom by his wonderful last
sacrifice. As a judge, he "worked righteousness" (that is, justice)
by righting wrongs, and exercising the judgments of God's Law.

He certainly "stopped the mouth of a lion" in the most
courageous manner. He escaped death—even of a thousand
Philistine swords, with only a donkey's jawbone as a weapon. At
that time, he became valiant in battle and turned to flight the
armies of the aliens.

After his fall, he did indeed endure torture with chains and
imprisonment and mockings in Dagon's temple. Samson was
tempted and ensnared by Delilah. He was destitute when he
hid in the rock at Etam, afflicted and tormented in the
dungeons of Gaza. Always pursued by the Philistines, he
wandered in deserts and mountains, in dens and caves of the
earth.

God gave him strength all his life but, for his final victory, it
was out of weakness that he was made strong.

The Spirit speaks of Samson among those "of whom the
world was not worthy."

Samson and us

There is no communication between the living and the dead.
Any that seek it have to endure the hurtful deceptions of the

Devil (Isa. 8:19-20). But that doesn't mean that there is no bond between Samson and us. He is with God now, awaiting the final stage of salvation, "the redemption of the body" (Rom. 8:23). He waits for the return of Jesus Christ and the resurrection of the body (1 Cor. 15:52-53).

That is why Hebrews 11 goes on to say that Samson and the others were not "made perfect apart from us" (v. 40). The children of God, whatever era they lived in, shall rise together on the last day.

Perhaps you will be standing next to him on that great day. Perhaps he will know of your trials and temptations, weaknesses and victories. Perhaps you will praise God together that He has made the weak strong.

Meanwhile, as the next verse (Heb. 12:1) says, "We are surrounded by so great a cloud of witnesses." What is meant by witnesses here? Certainly, it is true that Samson and the others have witnessed by living lives of faith. But the verse goes on to say: "Let us run with endurance the race that is set before us." The picture, therefore, is of a race, a sporting event.

The witnesses to sporting events are called "spectators." Not that Samson and the others know everything that goes on here on earth—only God is all-knowing. But it seems that the Spirit wants us to "run the race" with the encouragement of these heroic spectators.

Some years ago, I set aside an extended time for prayer. After spending a couple of hours with God, I realized that I was feeling very discouraged about my Christian life. The closer I came to the beauty of God, the uglier and more useless I felt. Discouragement threatened to overwhelm me.

Then I sensed that God wanted me to go up to the attic room of the house. I went up there and knelt before Him. Then a picture came to me of a runner in a race being cheered on by the crowds. The runner was covered with mud, exhausted, and soaked with perspiration—not a pretty sight! He had been battling through muddy fields and climbing obstacles. He felt so tired and was ready to give up, but the crowd wouldn't let him.

I realized that the runner was me—or you, or any Christian. The spectators were the witnesses of Hebrews 12:1, folk like Samson. Although they had all finished their course with honor, I remembered how many of them had slipped and fallen, as I had. They too had been covered with mud. They had felt utterly beaten, but had somehow kept going, and passed the winners' post.

It seemed to me that these heroes of faith would not be turning up their noses at me. Had I failed? Had I sinned? Had I been sickened by the betrayals of my flesh, and been ready to give up? So had they. It seemed that they were cheering me on. "Come on, Phil!" they shouted.

Of course, when you run this race, you will be covered with mud. You will be exhausted to the bone and long just to give up. This is a race, not an afternoon stroll. "Keep going!" they're telling you.

Our greatest comforts come from God. The Father knows how to bring us up to be like Himself. The Son has been a man on earth, and knows what it feels like. The Spirit lives within us and brings the love of Father and Son, with His own, right into our hearts. Yes, what wonderful comforts the children of God have in Him!

But Samson and other witnesses comfort us too. Unlike Jesus, they have sinned and failed. Their faith grew weak at times. They were a lot like us.

We shall one day be like them.

So, as we bid farewell to Samson, don't forget him. His story teaches us the secret of strength. He lives still, awaiting the same great day that we long for. And his great voice still thunders forth: "Keep going! Don't give up! You can make it!"

APPENDIX

Two major historical questions confront us when we look at the story of Samson. The first concerns the Philistines: Who were they, and how do they fit into ancient history? The second is a question of biblical chronology: How do Samson's and Samuel's stories fit together?

The Philistines in the flow of ancient history

If you look up "Philistines" in a standard Bible dictionary, you may well read that they were part of the "Sea People." As you read on, you find that the Sea People were a mysterious people from the general area of the Aegean. They attacked Egypt, we are told, and those who settled in Israel are Samson's Philistines. You are even shown a picture—Sea People in an ancient carving, wearing their distinctive "feathered crowns."

As you read, you are likely to become a little puzzled. Surely the Philistines were from Egypt (see Gen. 10:13-14)—not the Aegean? Furthermore, the Sea People weren't in Palestine in Abraham's time, but the Philistines were. How can that be explained? And why would conquerors from the Aegean speak Hebrew?

Something seems to be wrong. Why identify the Philistines with these Sea People? The answer lies with the orthodox dating of ancient history.

The orthodox ancient historian has his framework, and Christians are told to fit Bible events into it. Sometimes these events don't fit very easily. Orthodox historians, for instance, have Egyptian kings ruling before the birth of Mizraim, from whom all Egyptians were descended (Gen. 10:6). Christians, who know that the Bible is God's Word, know that this can't be right. We wonder where these historians get their time frame.

Amazingly, the orthodox time frame is based on very little solid data. Few hints and clues survive from ancient times, apart from the clear and reliable statements of the Bible. So, why base a time frame on these vague hints and then force the Bible into it? It is not as though the Bible has ever been proved to be unhistorical.

The problem, it seems, lies with humanism. The humanist is forced by his very beliefs to oppose the Bible. His whole faith is founded on the Bible being wrong, so how can he base his time frame on it?

But not all humanists are so consistent: there are some who have followed the facts, wherever they led.

Voices in the wilderness

Is it just Christians who oppose the modern time frame of ancient history? No. As we would expect, external evidence always ends up agreeing with the Bible. Although they don't believe the Bible to be God's Word, some humanistic historians have had the courage to speak up against the accepted scheme.

I say "courage," because humanists are never very happy to

hear something that threatens their beliefs and confirms the historicity of the Bible.

Beginning in 1952, Immanuel Velikovsky published a series of books under the general heading of *Ages in Chaos*. These challenged the accepted scheme of things, and examined the evidence against humanistic orthodoxy. Velikovsky's alternative scheme (which fits remarkably well with the Bible) was never disproved—but he himself was subject to a kind of persecution. His publisher was pressurized into withdrawing the books, and his views were outlawed.

The persecution failed. Velikovsky's books could not be suppressed, and continue to be read avidly. Although now dead, Velikovsky just won't go away. The books have been reworked by a Christian scholar (see Donovan Courville's *The Exodus Problem and Its Ramifications*, 2 volumes, Loma Linda, Challenge Books, 1971). The problems with the orthodox scheme are highlighted by yet another timescale. David Rohl (not, it seems, a believer) has produced an alternative to the accepted pattern, *A Test of Time* (Century, 1995).

It is not for us to judge between the rival schemes—perhaps an even better one is about to be produced. It is enough that we know the Bible is true and we cannot follow a scheme that assumes it is false.

Feathered crowns?

What about the Philistines' feathered crowns? They are strangely reminiscent of Persian helmets, of the fourth century, 800 years later. In fact, they are Persian helmets, according to Velikovsky (*Peoples of the Sea*, Abacus, 1977). Could their humanistic assumptions have led orthodox historians so far astray? Shouldn't we submit to the views of the orthodox humanistic experts?

Perhaps we should ask what Samson would have done. Would he have submitted to a Philistine interpretation of Israel's past? Would he have accepted their authority when the authority of God's Word was thereby slighted? Even if a thousand humanistic scholars had stood against him, Samson would have stood firm with his God. He might have asked how much the donkey's jawbone entered into what they were saying.

Anyway, rather than allow anything humanistic to enter our thinking on Samson, I have made no reference to any of the current theories. We have looked at the Bible alone, in its own terms.

There is an interesting book on the archeology of the Philistines, called *Giving Goliath His Due* (Neil Bierling, Baker Books, 1992). This follows the orthodox system of dating ancient history, so it is of limited use for our purposes. He demonstrates how little is known of the Philistines from the archeology of Palestine.

That leads us to the next question: How do Samson and Samuel fit together?

Samson and Samuel

Biblical chronology is fairly clear in its main features, but some minor parts create difficulties. One such difficulty is how to correlate the events of Judges with those of 1 Samuel. I have followed the traditional scheme.

The traditional scheme dovetails the end of Judges with the beginning of 1 Samuel. Judges narrates the beginning of the Philistine occupation; 1 Samuel its end. Neither book is complete without the other. Samson and Samuel were thus contemporaries. After Samson's untimely death, Samuel began his time as judge.

The traditional chronology is explained and defended in Keil's commentary on Judges (pp. 276–294, Keil & Delitzsch's *Commentary on the Old Testament*. Reprinted by Eerdmans,

1976). A similar line, more simply put, is found in Merrill's *Kingdom of Priests* (Baker, 1987), p. 173.

An alternative view has Samuel born after all the events of Judges. I have followed the traditional view without, of course, being absolutely able to prove it.

Commentaries on Judges

When you are born again, you find yourself belonging to a heavenly kingdom. You also find that you have joined a vast library! Believers from all centuries have left their God given wisdom behind in countless books.

So, if you want to go deeper into Samson, you need not limit yourself to modern books. In fact, it is better that you don't. Just because you and I live in the present day it doesn't mean that it is the wisest era. In fact, so far as knowing God's Word is concerned, we seem rather weak compared with recent centuries.

Here are some of the books I found helpful, with a few comments on their strengths.

Richard Rogers Commentary on Judges (1615)

Rogers, who describes himself as "preacher of God's word," is from that gifted era of Britain's seventeenth-century evangelicals usually known as Puritans. Many, like Rogers, combined virtues that are often separate today. They were profound scholars, and pastors and church-planters. They were experts on theology and familiar with the needs of the human soul. They believed everything in the Bible and lived holy lives. No wonder Jim Packer's book on them is called *Among God's Giants!*

Rogers' commentary is actually a sermon series, delivered in an age when Christians craved expert biblical preaching. As you read each verse, it is explained in its own terms, and enriched by insights from the whole Bible; it is applied to the human soul, and used to lead us directly into Christ's presence.

I found the "olde Englishe" a problem. In the only edition I know of (reprinted by the Banner of Truth, 1983), the book is in the original typeface. This makes reading very hard! The "s" is printed like an "f," the "v"s like "u"s, and it's very confusing. It was a real effort!—but worth the trouble.

Bishop Hall's Contemplations (17th century)
This isn't exactly a commentary; more a narration of the biblical stories. The bishop had wonderful insight and a strikingly beautiful writing style. It is frankly a pleasure to read him, and there are marvelous depths in his apparent simplicity.

John Milton's Samson Agonistes (1671)
Milton was the famous author of *Paradise Lost*. His dramatic poem on Samson is in the same style. It reflects the depth of Bible study for which his era is famous, but isn't an explanation of the Bible text. If you read it, I recommend you read it aloud, otherwise it loses its dramatic effect.

Matthew Henry's Commentary on the Whole Bible (1706)
What can I say about this ever popular treasure house? Christians wanting to meet God in His Word have always found this an enormous help. It combines all the strengths of the Puritan era which was then closing. If you want to seriously to study the Bible, and aren't allergic to old books, I really recommend Henry. Other favorite commentaries on the whole Bible from this era include Matthew Poole and John Gill.

Keil and Delitzsch on the Old Testament (19th century, reprinted currently by Hendrickson)
These two German evangelicals fought a losing battle as fash-

ionable unbelief was overwhelming German theology. Their commentary is very useful for the Hebrew reader, and full of academic observations. In this way, it supplements the more popular (and spiritual) style of Matthew Henry.

Keil covers Judges. He gives little clue to the spiritual riches in it, but is very helpful on the technical side.

A.R. Fausset on Judges (1885, reprinted by James and Klock, 1977)
Fausset is well known as a collaborator in the Jamieson, Fausset and Brown commentary on the Bible. His commentary on Judges is faithful and learned, but somehow doesn't come alive like the older commentaries do.

The Pulpit Commentary on the Whole Bible (19th century, reprinted by Hendrickson)
This style of commentary was highly popular at the end of the nineteenth century. The text is explained and then applied in sermon outlines. This double approach (explanation, then application) gives an opportunity to bring in all kinds of interesting observations. A similar approach was used by Lange in his *Bible Commentary* (reprinted by Zondervan in 1978) and the *Preacher's Homiletical Commentary*, neither of which are as good on Judges.

As you read these sets, you are definitely on a lower level than Matthew Henry and his era. The prevailing liberal humanistic theology made evangelicals a little embarrassed to be as spiritual as their forefathers. But, from time to time, some excellent remarks make it all worthwhile.

Judges—God's War Against Humanism by James Jordan (Geneva Ministries, 1985)
When I read a commentary, I want to be drawn closer to God.

I want to understand what *He* is saying in the Word. I want to know *Him*, what He has promised and what He commands. In the process, I expect to see myself in a clearer light. True theology is all about knowing God's love and loving Him. Without that, what's the point?

Why am I commending the older commentaries above the newer ones? I am very grateful to today's evangelical Bible commentators. They have labored under the dull shadow of "liberal" theology. Someone had to demonstrate—on every verse in the Bible—that the Bible really *is* God's Word. Twentieth-century evangelical scholars undertook this thankless task. I say "thankless," even though I (and many others) *do* thank them, because their success was so complete.

It wasn't long before they helped us see how empty and irrational humanism really is. We lost all patience with "liberal" theology. We had seen through their arguments, and consigned them to the realm of the irrelevant. We also grew tired of evangelical commentaries that constantly interacted with liberal views. We knew that the Bible is God's Word. We wanted to be led into its riches.

So, some of us put down our modern evangelical commentaries, and picked up Matthew Henry. But Jordan is one modern commentary that I found really stimulating. It would be impossible to agree with everything he says, but he is intensely interesting and remarkably creative. His main concern is to relate the sacred text to today's social situation (rather than our soul's needs). "What is God saying to the West through Judges?" he asks. He covers issues of modern society that the older writers couldn't address.

Have you enjoyed examining Samson and the secret of strength? Are there things you have seen which you hadn't seen when you read Judges on your own? It is wonderful to sit with the Holy Spirit and just read the Bible. But I have found many insights, made very real to me by the Holy Spirit, which I learned from the great masters of the Word.

Don't despise God's teachers—they have been given to us to equip us and build us up (Eph. 4:12). Thank God for each spiritual giant who, like Abel, "being dead, still speaks" (Heb. 11:4). When we have found the treasures in the church's library, we shall, like Paul, ask for "the books" (2 Tim. 4:13).

PERSONAL & GROUP STUDY GUIDE

Chapter 1
Riddle Upon Riddle

1. Read Judges 13–16. What is your first impression of Samson? Read Hebrews 11:32-39. How is Samson described in this passage? Does this description in Hebrews differ from your impression based on the passage in Judges? Discuss how Samson could be recognized in Hebrews as a hero of faith.
2. Even though Samson's life wasn't perfect, what aspects of his life can be an example for us to follow? Describe some concrete ways you can be like Samson—a hero of faith.
3. Compare and contrast Samson and King David. In what ways were they the same? In what ways were they different? Why do you think we see King David as more godly or holy than Samson?
4. Scripture says that the secret to Samson's strength was in his uncut hair. What do you think was really behind his strength? In what ways does the Holy Spirit give you strength?

Prayer Focus: Ask the Lord to reveal His strength in the areas of your life where you feel weak.

Chapter 2
The Importance of Being Different

1. How does the author compare Israel and the Philistines to Christians and humanists? List the ways that humanists and the Philistines are similar. List some humanistic philosophies that we accept in our society. What do we need to be cautious of concerning humanist philosophies?

2. The Philistines spoke the same language as Israel, making it even easier for the Philistines to influence the Israelites. How do humanists "speak the same language" as Christians?

3. The Philistines would not allow the Israelites to carry weapons. What "weapons" in our modern society seem to be dominated by the humanists and lacking in the Christian community?

4. Samson was different from other Israelites because of his Nazarite vow, and because he stood up against the Philistines. Compare Samson's situation to how Christians stand up against the world today. Discuss the opportunities you have to stand out from our non-Christian society. What lifestyle choices have you made that differ from the activities of our humanistic society?

5. Samson and Gideon's stories show us that when God's people are obedient then God's power is revealed. Do we see God's power revealed when we are obedient? Give examples.

6. Read Numbers 6. Discuss what was involved in being a Nazarite. The Nazarite vows were public displays of devotion to God. What are activities we do, clothes we wear, and things we say that publicly display our devotion to God? Sometimes it's difficult to publicly display our devotion to God, but as we face more and more persecution, we must commit to Jesus no matter the cost.

7. Samson's Nazarite vows strengthened his commitment to God, allowing God to use him. Have you made a commitment to righteousness? Are you willing to be used by God? Are you willing to make the vows required to be used by God? Discuss your answers to these questions.

Prayer Focus: Thank God for the opportunities He makes available in ministry. Ask Him for righteousness and humility in your life.

Chapter 3
First Strength

1. Read Judges 14:1-6. The Israelites went to battle with the Philistines without repenting for their sin. They lost the battle and the ark of the covenant. Sometimes we attempt to fight our battles without repenting our sin to God. Describe a time when your battle was lost because of unrepented sin.
2. Samuel and Samson were two men used by God to deliver Israel. List the similarities and differences between Samuel and Samson. Which attributes of these two men appeal to you? How could these attributes be effective in ministry?
3. Samuel and Samson were both Nazarites. Use a Bible dictionary, commentary, or concordance to list as many Nazarite vows and characteristics as you can. Discuss the vows you have made to God. What meaning do these vows bring to your life?
4. Discuss the "super gun" theory described in this chapter. How does it apply to Samuel and Samson? How does it apply to our churches today? Define what the "body of Christ" means to you. In what ways can we bring unity to the vast body of church denominations in our country?

5. "For God, faith is primarily linked with godliness." Do you agree or disagree with this statement? Using your concordance, look up Scripture that talks about faith and godliness. Be sure to read the context of these verses to get an indepth understanding of these two terms. With the research you've done, how does godliness and faith seem to be correlated? How do faith and godliness seem to be interrelated in your life?

6. The author challenges us to view Samson in a nontraditional perspective. Read Hebrews 11:32-34. What does Hebrews record about Samson? If Samson was a hero of faith and if faith requires godliness then Samson is recorded in Hebrews as godly. Discuss what you know about Samson and how he could have been counted as godly and righteous.

7. Read through the list of heroes of faith mentioned in Hebrews 11:32-34. List the various characteristics of these individuals. What common characteristics do these heroes of faith have according to the author? Which hero of faith do you relate to the most? Why?

8. What does the chapter say is the secret of Samson's strength? Read Matthew 5:6. Is this verse reflected in your life? Why or why not?

9. Why do you think Samson married a Philistine? Do you think Samson's marriage was God ordained? Discuss the three issues the chapter presents about Samson's marriage. Do you agree or disagree with these three points? Why or why not? Do you think God ordains circumstances in our lives that don't always make sense to us? Give examples of this in your life.

8. The Spirit of the Lord came on Samson and empowered him to kill the lion. How do we recognize the Holy Spirit's promptings and empowerment in our lives? Describe a situation when you felt prompted by the Holy Spirit. What did you do?

Prayer Focus: Meditate on Hebrews 11:32-34. Focus on the righteousness exemplified by the heroes of faith. Allow God to make you more righteous.

Chapter 4
The Sphinx Thinks

1. Samson married into the Philistine nation. We have to wonder if Samson was impacted by the Philistine ways. Discuss how Christians can be "in the world" but not "of the world." Christians should strive to impact the world with biblical truth and not be impacted by the world's pagan beliefs. Using Samson as an example, what are some ways we can we impact our world today?

2. List some biblical characters that were influenced by Israel, discovering a relationship with the living God. What factors were involved in bringing these people to God? How can we apply these factors to our own witnessing?

3. "Walking with God is a matter of constant miracles." Sharing these daily miracles with unbelievers is a subtle way to share the Gospel. What are some daily miracles you could share?

4. Do you believe that Creation is proof that God exists? Why or why not? List some characteristics of God that you see in Creation.

5. What are the arguments the author presents that prove God is the Creator? What are the opposing, humanistic arguments to God being the Creator? Do some role playing, one person presenting the God as Creator argument, one person presenting the humanistic argument.

6. God created the universe in such a way that He could be known to His Creation. Give some examples of ways that we come to know the Creator through the Creation.

7. Jesus' resurrection is a highly debated issue. Discuss the arguments the author presents to prove Jesus' resurrection. These arguments are useful in sharing the Gospel to your associates and friends. Read Matthew 28:16-20 and discuss opportunities you might have to fulfill Jesus' New Testament commission.

Prayer Focus: Thank God for His Creation. Mention specific parts of Creation that especially touch you. Ask God for strength to witness to unbelievers about Jesus.

Chapter 5
Initial Betrayal

1. Samson sought true love in his marriage to the Philistine woman. Discuss what you believe is true love. How does 1 Corinthians 13 define true love? Read 1 Corinthians 13 aloud. How does the definition of true love in 1 Corinthians 13 compare to your definition?
2. Unfortunately for Samson, his new wife betrayed him, leaving him for another man. Adultery is a rampant sin, and God knew the temptation we would face. So, He warned us against adultery in the Ten Commandments. What are some of the stumbling blocks that lead to adultery? In a Christian marriage, what do you think is the appropriate response to adultery? What does God allow for individuals whose spouses have commited adultery?
3. The '60s brought the sexual revolution. Now we live in a society tainted by sexual promiscuity and sexual disease. What should we tell the younger generation concerning the decisions they will have to make about sex? What should the Christian community do to educate children and teenagers

about these issues? What can we do as adults to show the younger generation how to live godly lives—even godly sexual lives?

4. "Wives submit to your husbands, as to the Lord. Husbands love your wives just as Christ also loved the church." Discuss what each of these portions of Ephesians means. How can wives submit? How should husbands love? Do we live this out in our marriages? Why or why not?

5. The Christian community is the world's only example of true godly love. Are we good examples? Why or why not? What can you do in your life to be a godly example of true love?

6. Samson's marriage failed. List the pointers the author gives to building a happy marriage. Discuss some other things you think could help build a happy marriage. Give personal examples if you have them.

Prayer Focus: Ask God to teach you how to truly love one another. Meditate on what Scripture defines as true love: that Christ died for us even while we were still sinners.

Chapter 6
True Justice

1. Samson was a judge over Israel. Discuss what it meant to be a judge over Israel. Do we have leaders in the religious community today that are like Samson, the judge? List some.

2. When the world sees true love in our lives, they see Christ in us. Discuss what true love is from a spiritual perspective. How do we express true love to God?

3. What does the author describe as "lawless love"? List some effects of lawless love. How can we turn lawless love into true love?

4. One way the author recommends to turn lawless love into true love is by voting for Christian leaders in our country. Do you agree or disagree? What are some other ways we can impact our communities toward true love?

5. Scripture records many accounts of God judging and punishing the nations for disobedience. Do you think our nation is being punished today? List the possible punishments our nation is facing.

Prayer Focus: Ask God to help you seek His Word to find true love rather than following your own idea of what it is.

Chapter 7
Valour's Finest Victory

1. How do you define courage? Name some of your heroes. In what ways was Samson a hero? By what power did Samson receive his courage? How can we receive this same courage?

2. True bravery comes from God. Describe a time that you received true bravery from God.

3. What do you think of the courage you have read about in this chapter? Do Samson and other biblical martyrs put us to shame? Are we prepared to die for God? Why or why not?

4. Cowardice comes from fear. What are some things you fear? Use your concordance to see what Scripture says about fear. How does the Scripture say we can overcome our fear?

5. Jesus calls us to be courageous like Samson. What daily situations do we face that require courage? Do you have courage to stand up for your beliefs and witness to nonbelievers?

Prayer Focus: Thank God for His power to overcome all fear through love. Meditate on the fear Jesus faced on the cross and the sacrifice He made for us despite His horrendous circumstances.

Chapter 8
The Prayer of Faith

1. When Samson prayed to God for water, God miraculously supplied it. Why didn't Samson just take water from the dead Philistines' water bottles? Samson's actions display moral courage, even righteousness. Do you think Samson's commitment to his Nazarite vow had anything to do with why God supplied him with water? Why or why not?

2. Samson's request for water could only have been granted by a miracle of God. Have you ever asked God for something as big as Samson asked for? What was it? When you asked, did you expect to have your prayer answered? Why or why not?

3. When we pray we should follow Samson's example. What three things did Samson do in order that his prayer was answered? In your prayer life, do you practice these three things? Do you think God would empower you if you followed Samson's example? Why or why not?

4. Why are obedience and answered prayer so dependent on each other? Do you see a pattern in your life reflecting answered prayer because of obedience to God? Explain.

5. Samson gave glory to God in his prayer. Do you make a practice of giving glory to God for the blessings in your life? What about giving Him glory for the lessons you learn? What about giving Him glory in your suffering? Discuss some of the circumstances in your life where you need to give glory to the Lord. Praise Him aloud right now.

6. We must realize God is the source of strength in our lives. Describe a time when you took credit for something you should have attributed to God.

7. Sometimes it's difficult to give up our pride and give up trying to control our lives. Define humility. How should we

have humility before God?

8. We should always pray for God's will in our lives. Do you find this difficult to do? Why or why not? Consider the story of Job. After everything that happened to Job, what did he say even to the end? (See Job 42:1-6.) Do you think you could be as faithful as Job? As faithful as Samson? Why or why not?

Prayer Focus: Come humbly before the Lord. Make sure you are completely obedient to His will and give Him glory. Then ask for something big.

Chapter 9
Twenty Years On

1. Define temptation. What does temptation lead to? How can we overcome temptation? What temptation did Samson face in Gaza? What was the outcome? How should Samson have dealt with his temptation differently?

2. The author theorizes that Samson became prey to temptation because what made Samson strong also made him weak. Do you agree or disagree? Have you ever felt isolated because of your religious vows and beliefs? Have you ever felt different because of the Christian lifestyle you live? Has it ever made you doubt why you are a Christian? Maybe this is how Samson felt.

3. Augustine said pride is the basis of all sin. Martin Luther said sin is unbelief. Which do you think it is? Why?

4. How are we saved from our sin? Do we sometimes try to take control of our lives after we've already given it over to God? Describe a time when you tried to take your life out of God's hand and do it yourself. How can we give up our pride and humble ourselves before God?

5. Discuss what the author describes as the fundamental truth of humility. How does humility draw us closer to God? Have you experienced humility before God? Explain.
6. How does complete humility allow us to trust ourselves fully to God? What have we given ourselves in comparison to what God has given us? The cross is the best place to go to learn humility.

Prayer Focus: Practice humility as you pray to God.

Chapter 10
Final Betrayal

1. Why did Samson never cut his hair? To cut his hair or allow someone else to cut his hair would have been disobedience to God. What are vows that we make that would be disobedience if we broke them?
2. Why was Samson breaking his vow to allow Delilah to cut his hair, but not breaking his vow when the Philistines forcibly shaved his head? Why did the Lord take Samson's strength away? Have you ever felt as if the Lord had left you because of your disobedience? Explain.
3. What does Paul teach us about in 2 Corinthians 12:1-10? Paul talks about a "thorn" that kept him humble. Do you ever experience a "thorn" in your life? Do you struggle with pride? Explain.
4. Even though temptation of the flesh plagues us, who is always with us to defeat temptation? Have you ever been able to relate with Paul in that "what I will to do, that I do not practice; but what I hate, that I do"? Explain.
5. How do Samson's circumstances parallel what Paul wrote about? Paul, Samson, and us today all deal with temptation

and failure. But "My grace is sufficient for you, for my strength is made perfect in weakness." List some other biblical characters who were made perfect in their weakness. Can you also relate to this verse? Explain.

6. Could it be that God would deliver Israel from the Philistines in spite of Samson's total weakness? How does the story of Samson end? Was God's purpose fulfilled? Has God used you even in your weakness?

Prayer Focus: Ask the Lord to teach you humility and use you in your weakness.

Chapter 11
Sundown

1. What did Samson pray as he was bound before the Philistines? God heard Samson's prayer. What does this teach us about God's love? Discuss the times when God has shown you unconditional love.

2. Sometimes we take for granted the blessings God gives us. Maybe Samson had taken for granted his strength. Take a minute to list some daily blessings that you take for granted. Remember to pray, thanking the Lord for these blessings.

3. What are the two things the author says we can learn from Samson's prayer? How can we be active in making our country just and righteous? "We must remember that God's Law is His will." Do we fulfill God's will? The place to start is by obeying His commands.

4. When Samson cried, "Let me die!" he joined a select group of Bible heroes. List some other Bible characters who gave their lives in martyrdom. Discuss the various reasons why these heroes gave their lives. There are those who die in

today's world in Christ's name. Are you prepared to die for your faith? Why or why not?

5. Samson's death and the circumstances of his story all seem to make sense—to be part of God's ultimate plan. Do you sometimes see a glimpse of God's plan in your life? Describe a time when God may have revealed His plan to you. How does it make you feel to know that God has a plan for you?

6. Did Samson learn the secret of his strength? Of course the secret was not in Samson's long hair. Where does our strength come from? Maybe we're not facing 1,000 armed men or lions or deceitful women, but we do face work and kids, finances and relationships. Discuss how you gain the strength for your daily battles.

Prayer Focus: Thank Jesus for His ultimate sacrifice. Petition Him for the strength you need realizing that He may request some sacrifice from you.

Chapter 12
Aftermath

1. "God always wins, and we always win in Him." Do you agree or disagree? Explain. Sometimes it doesn't seem like God wins until a long time later. Sometimes it seems that God could never win considering the circumstances. Describe a time when you weren't sure if God was going to win the battle in your life.

2. What is God's revealed will? What is His secret will? How does evil play a role in God's will? Define free will. What does free will allow humans to do? How does free will make true love for God possible?

3. In Samson's story all things worked together for the good.

How could this be true? Even though Satan tries to make everything evil, God can still have His will done. Have you ever experienced a time when God's will was fulfilled despite the evil or sinful circumstances? Describe.

4. In the early church suffering made the Christians stronger. What are some of the persecution and suffering endured by Christians today? Have you experienced any persecution or suffering? Do you agree that persecution and suffering make the church stronger? Why or why not?

5. Sometimes, like Augustine, we have to experience sin in our lives before we can draw close to God. Do you agree or disagree? Why or why not?

6. What are some of the things Samson did that are listed in Hebrews 11:33-38? After completing this study of Samson, how do you view Samson? Do you still think of him as a failed man of God who lost his strength in disobedience and died in ruin? Or do you see him as a hero of faith—blessed by God yet broken down by temptation and weakness?

7. Is Samson an encouragement to you? Do you believe that God can use you even in your weakness? Discuss the significant points this study has taught you about yourself.